BY PHYLLIS ROSE

Woman of Letters: A Life of Virginia Woolf

Parallel Lives: Five Victorian Marriages

Writing of Women: Essays in a Renaissance

Jazz Cleopatra: Josephine Baker in Her Time

Never Say Goodbye: Essays

NEVER

SAY

GOODBYE

NAN A. TALESE

DOUBLEDAY

New York   London   Toronto   Sydney   Auckland

NEVER
SAY
GOODBYE

ESSAYS BY

PHYLLIS
ROSE

PUBLISHED BY DOUBLEDAY

a division of
Bantam Doubleday Dell Publishing Group, Inc.
666 Fifth Avenue, New York, New York 10103

DOUBLEDAY *and the portrayal of an anchor*
with a dolphin are trademarks of
Doubleday, a division of Bantam Doubleday Dell
Publishing Group, Inc.

The essays in this volume originally appeared in the following
publications: the New York Times, *the* New York Times
Magazine, *the* Hartford Courant, Vogue, Iowa Review,
The Atlantic, New England Monthly, Glamour, *and*
Lear's.

Typography and binding design by Marysarah Quinn

Library of Congress Cataloging-in-Publication Data
Rose, Phyllis
Never say goodbye : essays / by Phyllis Rose.—1st ed.
p.   cm.
I. Title.
AC8.R599   1991
081—dc20   90-37827
CIP

FOR TEDDY

·CONTENTS·

CYCLE I · NEW YORK

CYCLE II · FRANCE

CYCLE III · NEW ENGLAND

NEVER
SAY
GOODBYE

CYCLE · I

NEW

YORK

CUT DOWN TO SIZE

Once I tried to find a hairdresser less expensive than the one I usually use. Calling in August, I got an appointment in late October. My hair grew. Ends split. Eventually I drove the two hours from my home to Manhattan.

My appointment was for noon. I changed into the salon smock and read a magazine. At 12:05, the receptionist told me that Roger had called on his car phone: stuck in traffic, he would be a little late.

He was only fifteen minutes late. Richard regularly kept me waiting half an hour, sometimes an hour, with no apology. If Roger got in his car and circled the block in order to call a new client on the car phone and put her in a state of abjection, he needn't have bothered. I felt abject as all get-out in that awful smock, unprotected by my own clothes, my hair almost as blond as a Barbie doll's and seeming both to frizz and hang limply to midneck.

Roger said, "Too bad you've changed. I like to see my clients in their own clothes first, to get a sense of their style." A good-looking man with blue eyes and dark hair, he eyed me with distaste. "But I must tell you, I'd be very surprised if I end up cutting your hair."

That, I supposed, was a joke, so I joked in return: "My clothes are hanging in the closet. You can take a look at them if you like."

"Good idea," he said solemnly. I led him to my clothes. He looked, and then, like a young knight in a fairy tale required to make love to a hideous hag, brought me to his chair before the mirror.

I said, "Judith suggested I come to you."

"Judith's hair is typical of the work I do."

"I like Judith's hair. That's why I'm here."

"Judith's hair is healthy."

"Oh, I see," I said. "You're not into damaged hair."

"No," he said, holding a strand or two of my hair distantly, as though it were blue spaghetti. "I'm not. Overworked color like yours—well, I only like it when it's intended to be amusing. We might have tried to bring it back, but you've taken it too far. I'd be very surprised if I could cut your hair. Didn't you come in for a consultation? That's why I like to do consultations."

"No one said anything about a consultation. I've waited three months for this appointment." Tears were coming to my eyes, and I had no privacy. There were clients on my left and right and hairdressers at work on them, pretending not to listen. "I drove two hours to get here."

"Well, I drove in, too," he said. "I tell you what:

we'll wash out your conditioner"—pronounced to mean *inferior, second-rate product*—"and see what we have then."

I summoned up my last bit of self-esteem and said, "It doesn't sound as if it's worth the trouble. You don't seem to like anything about my hair."

"No," said Roger. "I don't." And so I walked out, and managed not to start crying until I hit Seventh Avenue.

The French have a phrase to describe the things you should have said but didn't have the presence of mind to say at the time, the things you thought of as you left the scene of confrontation—*l'esprit d'escalier*, staircase wit. Many friends later helped me come to terms with my humiliation by contributing pieces of staircase wit. "Who do you think you are? Picasso?" was a favorite. The best was from a man who refused to believe that Roger liked women, and I will give only an expurgated version: "If you think this is bad, you should see me naked."

My mother, who is old school and thinks of hair-dressers as servants and employees rather than artists and professionals, was horrified that I took this insult from an underling. What kind of spineless creature had she spawned? Another friend echoed her: "Who would have thought you were so passive?"

Most of my friends seemed to think they could have handled it better than I did, and I'm sure they were right. One insinuated that it served me right for being so elitist as to go to New York to get my hair cut. However much it shook my confidence, the incident did me no harm with my acquaintances. Envy is the only dangerous feeling to provoke. Giving people a chance to patronize you every once in a while only increases their affection.

I saw a woman humiliated by a hairdresser in Paris. It wasn't a pretty sight. I saw her come into the salon proud, strong, self-confident, and leave like a whipped dog. An American, she had come to Paris all the way from Germany, where she was living, because she didn't trust the Germans to do her hair.

She had grown it for years so that it could be cut straight across the bottom, as was then being done in New York. The Parisian hairdresser began to layer it. The proud woman winced and tried to object. The hairdresser said, "I cannot cut your hair unless you have confidence in me." After that, the woman quivered and watched without protest as her hair was ruined. When the hairdresser stepped away for a moment, she broke into tears and I tried to comfort her. We both agreed that the worst part was, French women looked good. Why couldn't we?

At that moment I realized what a complex cultural achievement a haircut is, the product not only of a sophisticated negotiation between hairdresser and client but of subtle, culturally coded understandings of identity and status. As an American, I could see this was a woman to be reckoned with, but the French hairdresser did not. Treated as though she were contemptible, she soon became so.

The haircut I got that day was equally poor. Later I learned from a journalist friend what I had to do to get my hair cut well in Paris. I had to explain very carefully that I was a writer and that I wanted *un look Colette*. Otherwise the hairdresser, unable to place me, would do a second-rate assembly-line haircut.

I think that no man would stand for the treatment from a barber that women often get from hairdressers. Perhaps the low-cost haircut is men's secret source of strength. I know a very successful lawyer who clings to the cheap barbers in Grand Central Terminal with moral fervor, as though to give in to the pressures to get an eighty-dollar haircut were to begin down a path that leads inevitably to insider trading. He may be right. For women, however, I would argue that moral strength lies on the side of the expensive—or at any rate abusive—haircut. My experience with Roger is the kind that keeps you humble, makes you a kinder person, prevents you from misusing your own power, holds arrogance at bay. If the seven-dollar haircut fosters ascetic idealism in men, the hundred-dollar haircut and its attendant humiliations keep well-heeled women attuned to the plight of the scorned and unfortunate.

The afternoon of my humiliation by Roger, I was lucky enough to get an appointment with my darling Richard. He ran his fingers unhesitatingly through my bleached-out strands and said, "I love your hair." "You do? Really?" I said, with pathetic gratitude. I would never try to leave him again. I would put up with his little weaknesses, like charging too much. "Yes, I really love it," he said. I should have been reassured, my ego re-inflated, but instead I said to myself, "Richard must be into damaged hair."

OF SHARED
MEMORIES

My mother has always said, "The daughters come back to you eventually. When the sons go, they're gone." She has other favorite sayings—"A father's not a mother," "The beginning is half of all things," and *"De gustibus non disputandum est,"* which she translates as "That's what makes horse races"—all of which have become increasingly meaningful to me with time. Recently I told her that she was right in a fight we had twenty-seven years ago about which language I should study in high school. This came up because I had just had the same discussion with my son and took the side my mother took then (French). She laughed when I told her that she had been right twenty-seven years earlier. There have been more and more nice moments like that with my mother as we both grow older.

She is seventy-five, ash blond, blue-eyed, a beauty. When my father died three years ago she suddenly developed glaucoma and lost a lot of her vision. She says she literally "cried her eyes out." She can read only very slowly, with the help of a video enhancer supplied by the Lighthouse, the New York Association for the Blind. Nevertheless, her lipstick is always perfect. She doesn't use a mirror. She raises her hand to her lips and applies it. When I praise her for this, she says, "By now I should know where my mouth is."

She doesn't walk alone at night and during the day rarely gets beyond the area she can reach on foot, between Fiftieth and Sixtieth streets, First Avenue and Fifth. She loves to transgress those boundaries, so when I come in from Connecticut I usually pick her up in my car and drive her to distant parts of Manhattan: the Lower East Side, the Seaport, TriBeCa, SoHo, the Village. One of our favorite things to do together is to have Sunday brunch at a restaurant on West Broadway near Houston Street. We go there especially for the pecan pancakes and the scrambled eggs with salmon and dill.

One day this winter we went there for Sunday brunch. It was a particularly cold day and I was suffering from a pulled muscle in my neck. I walked with one shoulder higher than the other. My mother walked slowly and with a slight stoop. But as soon as we entered the door, the restaurant buoyed us up. We were patrons, to be pampered. We had a reservation. We could share in the general atmosphere of youth, energy, chic, competence, success. The waiters were stylishly dressed with an accent of the 1940s. This was SoHo.

One young man, wearing a plaid shirt and pinch-pleated trousers, showed us a table in a bright front section overlooking the sidewalk. This was excellent for my mother, who often finds restaurants too dark and carries a spelunker's light to read menus by. But we didn't need a menu; we ordered pecan pancakes and scrambled eggs with salmon and dill. When they arrived we split them and I began with the eggs. "Eat the pancakes first," my mother said. I didn't ask why. She's my mother. She has to tell me how to do things.

Three beautiful women dressed in black who were eating lunch at a table nearby finished eating, cleared their table, and moved it aside. From the corner they took a cello, a violin, and a flute, removed their covers, and positioned themselves to play. They started with Schubert and went on to a medley of Strauss waltzes. My spirits soared. I looked at my mother to see if she was listening to the music. She was. I could see she was as ravished by it as I was, and for the same reason. Without exchanging a word, both of us moved simultaneously thirty years backward in our minds and to another place.

"Palm Beach," I said.

My mother nodded. "Hoops, crinolines, strapless dresses with net skirts, white fox stoles. Each of us took three suitcases. Those days are gone forever."

In the 1950s my father, in his proud and powerful middle age, took my mother, my brother, my sister, and me to Palm Beach for two weeks every winter until just after New Year's Day. We stayed at a hotel called the Whitehall; its core was originally the mansion of Henry M. Flagler, the railroad man and Florida pioneer. The lobby had floors of inlaid marble and variegated marble pillars.

The Whitehall dining room was a gigantic sunken area that, family legend said, was Mr. Flagler's indoor swimming pool. Whether it was or not didn't matter then, doesn't now. It was a magical place. The families as they came in for dinner and took their usual places were brilliantly dressed: fathers in the light-colored raw silk jackets appropriate for the South; mothers in strapless dresses with wide skirts supported by hoops and crinolines; children, after a day on the beach and the tennis courts, scraped, peeling, but burnished for dinner. Nothing was casual. The hotel hairdresser was heavily booked. Elaborate sets and comb-outs several times a week were not unusual. Jewelry was not left in the vault at home. The room sparkled. There was general splendor, the result of all that effort and the discipline of dressing for dinner. And at the center of the room a quintet in black formal clothes played music throughout the four-course meal. Every night, usually during the clear consommé, they played a medley of Strauss waltzes.

My mother and I are tied together because we share the same memories. My brother and sister share them, too. We are a family because the Whitehall, a certain dude ranch in the Great Smokies, the layout of our house on Central Avenue, and other recondite geographies exist in our minds and in no others. We move in the same mental spaces. In some of our dreams we wander the same streets, trying to get back to the same house. One form of loneliness is to have a memory and no one to share it with. If, in twenty years, I want to reminisce about Sunday brunch in a certain SoHo restaurant, I may have nobody to reminisce with. That will be lonely.

Often I feel I do not do enough for my mother. When I read *King Lear* I realize that I'd be flattering myself to identify with Cordelia. I have the awful suspicion that I am much more like Regan or Goneril— from Lear's point of view, monsters of ingratitude;

from their own, just two women taking their turn at the top, enjoying their middle-aged supremacy. When these guilty thoughts afflict me, a folk tale comes to mind.

There once was a bird with three young to carry across a river. She put the first on her back and, halfway across, asked, "Will you care for me in my old age as I have cared for you?" "Yes, Mama," said the first bird, and the mother dumped him in the river, calling him liar. Second bird, same result. "Will you care for me in my old age as I have cared for you?" "Yes." "Liar." But the third bird, asked if he would care for his mother in her old age as she had cared for him, answered: "I can't promise that. I can promise only to care for my own children as you have cared for me."

It's a truthful response and it satisfied the mother bird, a philosophic spirit if ever there was one. But when I imagine my son saying the same thing to me— "I can promise only to care for my own children as you cared for me"—I don't seem to find much comfort in it.

SURVIVING
SUCCESS

Things have been going well for me recently. I've been on a roll. You'd think this would make me happy, but I'm superstitious. I believe someone up there keeps track and allows only a certain amount of good luck. At any moment I expect to be hit by a tidal wave of misfortune. Recently my son, playing at school, hurt his knee—painfully but not seriously, as it turned out. When he called to tell me, I wasn't surprised; something like that was bound to happen. Teddy and I got off easily—this time.

Believing that we are entitled only to a certain amount of good fortune is enough to neutralize some of the pleasure of good fortune when it comes. But it's also true that good news doesn't stay with you minute to minute the way bad news does. Let's say you get a promotion. This makes you very happy for as much as a couple of days. You celebrate. You drink champagne. But you don't get up every succeeding morning elated, saying to yourself:,"Whoopee! I've been promoted." You spend up to your emotional income; you come to depend on the degree of satisfaction that being promoted gives you. A colleague said of his promotion, "The most fleeting pleasure I've ever had." Compare the experience of being fired. You live with that misery day after day. It darkens every morning, makes you feel—like the loss of someone you love—that you've been socked in the stomach every time you think of it.

Success in work, like success in love, breeds disquieting questions that failure does not. Success leads you to ask yourself if you really want the thing you have pursued so hard and finally obtained. Twenty years from now will you still want to be in this job? This marriage? Failure often gives you energy to fight and leaves you with the comforting illusion that success is beautiful and worth pursuing. Success, on the other hand, tends to engender depression. What you've got doesn't seem as good as you thought it would be. All that energy—for this?

When I've been down, people have helped me; when I'm up, they assume I don't need kindness. A publisher rejected my first book at a particularly bad moment. My colleagues were uniformly sympathetic: one advised me to get drunk; several reassured me that the manuscript was good; two actually helped me to place it. When your work is regularly published, your friends don't bother anymore to tell you it's good; they suppose that it goes without saying. If anything, they may think that you need taking down a peg or that they have a responsibility to point out your flaws.

I'm sure the same is true in other professions. Competence is expected. At a certain point you can only stumble. Who praises the dentist for doing a good filling? Who congratulates the surgeon for performing a successful operation? Who thanks the accountant for filling out the tax return with no mistakes? But if the filling falls out, the scalpel slips, or the math falters, we notice and complain. When I first started teaching at Wesleyan University, the president sent out letters at the end of the academic year thanking the faculty for having performed its duties responsibly. This lovely but superfluous and no doubt expensive gesture has of course disappeared.

Have you noticed that we discount praise but register criticism full strength? I, for example, am subjected to evaluations of my teaching that students turn in at the end of every course. If they're enthusiastic, they don't seem enthusiastic enough. The words of praise evaporate, whereas barbs from 1971 stay in my mind with the power to wound. The nasty people seem to have X-ray vision into my soul. The kindly ones seem to be writing about someone else or not to be looking very hard.

You might think that people become more self-confident as they become more successful, but this isn't always true. Successful people (men as well as women) have confided to me that it gets harder, not easier, the more established they are. No one understands that they can still be apprehensive about failing and that they now have farther to fall. They're afraid they've had their last idea, written their last paragraph, made their last deal.

My friend Annie Dillard was washing lettuce when she learned that she had won the Pulitzer Prize. The man telephoning her said, "What are you doing right this moment?" "Washing lettuce," she said. "Don't you realize this means you'll never have to wash lettuce again?" Nonsense. The lettuce always has to be washed.

In the inner life, as in the kitchen, little changes. Many people assume that everything has changed for you with success, so you can easily feel misunderstood. You may be tempted to start acting as people expect you to act, like a person who never has to wash lettuce. You develop a public persona.

If people like your public persona, you may feel that they do not like "the real you" or that they do not like you for your "self." Whatever that elusive entity is— "self" or "real you"—it is deeply buried, not visible to the public. It is not how you look or how you lecture or how you write, and although it's hard to put your finger on what it is, it's what you want to be loved for. Usually it's exactly the thing that is not obvious about you. I asked a perky woman administrator what she wanted to be loved for and she promptly said, "My dark side." She certainly didn't want to be loved for what she had accomplished. Work and love are two satisfying things, but just as few people want to gain professional success as a favor from a loved one, few people want to be loved for how well they do their work.

Men seem more bound to the wheel of success than women do. That women are trained to get satisfaction from affiliation rather than achievement has tended to keep them from great achievement. But it has also freed them from unreasonable expectations about the satisfactions that professional achievement brings. No doubt, as women move more and more into the professions on an equal basis, they will be as suckered by success as men are.

I asked the students in my course on Touchstones

of Western Values to write a Socratic dialogue. What usually happens in a Socratic dialogue is that someone who professes to believe in something—virtue or piety, for example—runs into Socrates, who makes it clear that the concept is meaningless or that the believer, at any rate, has no idea what it means. Most of my students wrote dialogues in which young people discovered the hollowness of the concept success. These are highly motivated students who know they are expected to get "success," but they are not sure they know what it is or if they really want it. Smart people. Later, when they have made an investment in this or that kind of success, it will be harder to afford such skepticism.

All of which is not to say that we should go out looking for failure and misfortune. No need to. They will probably find us soon enough.

TALKING IT OUT

My twelve-year-old son just walked into my study on the verge of tears. He and his best friend, Ian, had a fight. Ian stormed away on his bicycle. Teddy didn't think this was fair. He wanted a chance to explain himself and "talk it out," although when I asked him what the fight was about, he couldn't remember.

Wherever Teddy got the idea that you should "talk things out," it wasn't from me. I favor reticence, silence, discretion—and action. I told Teddy perhaps Ian was right to go away. Often after a fight people are best off separating and giving each other time to get over it. He and Ian have been friends too long for anything to end their friendship. This cloud would pass.

But Teddy would not be soothed. "Ian went home," he said. "The afternoon is shot."

"So get on your bike and go after him. Say you're sorry, forget the whole thing, and have a nice afternoon."

Just then the doorbell rang.

"Maybe it's Ian, coming back to make up with you," I said.

And to Ian's credit, it was.

Many fights come about because we use speech badly: to wound others, to defend ourselves, to flatter ourselves, to express what we wish were true but isn't, to convince ourselves that we are not as confused as we are—and because the realities we want to express are elusive. Why do we think we can use speech any better to work out the damage that speech has caused? Other fights result from people's irreconcilable differences of interest or style. What often happens in "talking out" such a disagreement is that one person eventually agrees to abdicate his or her position. But the abdication is strategic and temporary. The difference of interests or styles reasserts itself, and nothing has been worked out.

I believe in saying clearly what one thinks, trying to describe what one feels when that's useful, keeping quiet often, and being lavish with flattery. I believe in talking, but that's not the same thing as talking things out, a ritual of the progressive and hopeful view of human communication. In the tragic view, people speak essentially in monologues. Listeners get from these monologues what is useful to them, often the opportunity to begin a monologue of their own.

In *The Book of Laughter and Forgetting*, Milan Kundera discusses a phrase much used in conversation as a transition: "That's just like me, I . . ." This phrase might seem a way of advancing an idea by agreement and expansion, but it is really "an attempt to free one's ear from bondage." Kundera writes that "all man's life among men is nothing more than a battle for the ears of others." No doubt I am more skeptical than most people about "talking things out" because I am bad at this form of combat. I forget the main points for the qualifications and complexities. I capitulate quickly. I feel easily bullied by someone else's fluency.

If "talking things out" is disguised combat, a related fallacy is the healthiness of "expressing your anger." Recent studies have shown that expressing your anger may be less purgative than we have been led to believe. It acts rather as a confirmation. People who express their anger a lot feel angrier more of the time. Science, in showing us this, has struck another blow for silence and civilized behavior.

When I concentrate on conveying information clearly in speech, I'm amazed at how little gets through—how crude my messages are. I remember once talking on the telephone for ten minutes, trying to give my response to the good news that something I'd written was going to be published. At the end of my ten-minute monologue, the editor I was speaking to said, with an air of great discovery, "I can sense that you're happy about this." At least the point got across, however inefficiently. And there were other points I was glad had not got across (which is probably why I took so long to say I was happy), including my humiliating fear that the news was not true.

Many spoken sentences result from complicated negotiations between wanting to be understood and not wanting to be understood too well. As a friend of mine asked: "How long do you think most couples would stay together if they knew absolutely everything that went on in each other's minds? Fifteen minutes?"

If there's anything people want more than to tell you—in the way that they want to tell you—what they're like, it's to *be* told what they're like. And people are so complex, containing so many possibilities and conflicting ideas of themselves, that almost anything you tell them about themselves is true. Hence the popularity of horoscopes. A French psychologist, as an experiment, advertised himself as an astrologer and sent the same generalized horoscope to all the people who wrote to him. He got two hundred letters praising his insight.

As an amateur reader of tarot cards, I know this from my own experience. People want the chaos of their lives shaped into some kind of meaning. When I tell them, "You have been disappointed in love" or "You are in conflict," I am always astounded by their looks of amazement and gratitude. People are hungry for personalized narratives, and any fortuneteller, viewed sympathetically, is a provider of useful and potentially valid plots.

Years ago, when I was married, childless, and spending the summer in London, I went to a palm reader in Battersea Park. More precisely, I went to Battersea Park, found myself—with my husband—in front of a palm reader's tent, and decided to enter. There was a line, but it moved quickly. The reading didn't cost much. Something like $1.50 for one palm, $3.00 for two. I had a two-palm reading. It was just a lark. I didn't think there was anything I particularly wanted to know.

The reader studied my palms and told me many vague and general things that I've forgotten. Then she told me I would have two children. Evidently, my face lit up. She added quickly, "But whether natural or adoptive I cannot say." I could feel my disappointment. I really hadn't known until that moment how much I wanted to have children.

When the general reading was over, the palm reader asked if I had any particular questions for her. At first I said no. Then something occurred to me. "I haven't been sleeping well recently," I said. "I think something's bothering me. I wonder if you could tell me what it is." She said, "I can see you're an American, love. In this country we have something wonderful called National Health. You go to a doctor before you go home and get him to give you a prescription for sleeping pills. It won't cost a penny."

This woman has stayed in my mind as a model of excellent therapy. She led me to know things about myself I hadn't known, and she gave me good advice. Most important, she distinguished between things worth looking into and things best dealt with by action. When I left, I wasn't surprised to see that the line of people waiting outside the tent to consult her had grown even longer.

BALANCING ACTS

A friend asked me to explain why she had seen *Coming Home* eight times. *Coming Home* is the film in which Jane Fonda plays the wife of a macho Marine officer. While he is serving in Vietnam she falls in love with a disaffected Vietnam veteran, paralyzed from the waist down. I asked my obsessed friend if she had liked *Jane Eyre* and if she was aware of the appeal of a wounded man. She saw the connection.

Charlotte Brontë, in her 1847 novel, spoke to the female fantasy of caring for a wounded man. Jane Eyre, an unloved orphan, works as a governess in the gloomy mansion of the mysterious and attractive Edward Rochester. They fall in love and, against all odds, he proposes marriage. At the altar, dreadful news is revealed: Mr. Rochester already has a wife and a legally binding marriage. Although his wife is insane, he may not remarry. Jane Eyre flees the intended bigamist and finds herself a home elsewhere. But she can't get Rochester out of her mind and returns to him to find that his wife had started a fire in which she was killed, the house destroyed, and Rochester blinded and maimed. He and Jane live happily ever after.

Why is the conclusion of *Jane Eyre* so satisfying? What is the nature of the wounded man's appeal to women? Is it a sadistic desire to see men suffer?

Luis Buñuel's film *Belle de Jour* provides an even more upsetting version of the fantasy of the wounded male. (This is the best film I know about several female sexual fantasies.) Catherine Deneuve plays an upper-class Parisian married to a successful surgeon. She seems to have everything—looks, money, a terrific husband—but apparently she wants something else, for she takes a job working afternoons in a brothel. One of her clients, a gangster, follows her home and shoots her husband in an attempt to get her for himself. But Belle de Jour, demurely dressed in black, stays by her crippled and blinded husband. She looks disturbingly happy as she pilots his wheelchair around their elegant apartment.

Is she glad her husband is hurt? Or is she glad that she's now the pilot? I think that in *Belle de Jour, Coming Home*, and *Jane Eyre*, the man's injury encourages a redistribution of power between a man and a woman. The women take to it.

Let me give another kind of example. John L. Michela, a psychologist formerly at Columbia University, discovered to his surprise that marriages generally improve after husbands suffer heart attacks. In a 1981 study, he interviewed married couples about a year after the husbands had had heart attacks and found that most of the couples reported that the marriages had improved. Professor Michela concluded—blandly, I think—that "marriages can get better if you learn that you love your partner and your partner loves you."

His findings may be another mystery best solved by invoking the fantasy of the wounded man. The husbands' illnesses may have initiated a change in the balance of power between marriage partners. Initially the women in the study were "anxious, angry, depressed," no doubt resenting the unfamiliar position of responsibility into which their husbands' misfortunes had thrust them. But most seem to have found new sources of vigor and satisfaction in the situation.

Many marriages still assume that the woman is the weaker partner and the man her protector. But women, like other human beings, have formidable resources of strength, which they rejoice in deploying and not all of which are mobilized by taking care of children. Some women may need permission to be strong and to take pleasure in their own strength. The illness of their male partners may give them this license to thrive.

On the other hand, some men may have to be in some way disabled to reconcile themselves to their wives' power. A striking finding in the study of contemporary couples by Philip Blumstein and Pepper Schwartz (*American Couples*, 1983) is the intensity with which men resent and are made uncomfortable when their wives earn more money than they do. This tangible sign of their wives' power is a blow to their masculine identity. But if a man is ill or wounded, he too may have permission to enjoy his wife's strength and to allow himself some weakness. If it's a drag for women always to have to be weak, it must be equally a drag for men always to have to be strong.

A man's wounds can be metaphorical—handicaps, in the sense in which golfers are given handicaps to equalize tournaments. Men were expected to enter marriage with a surplus or advantage: they were supposed to be older, taller, richer, and more successful than the women they married. Women were supposed, in every way, to look up to the men they married. The absence of one of these advantages—age, height, money, success—constitutes a handicap as I am using the word. Power has always been appreciated as a turn-on to women, but the absence of power in a man may be equally attractive. Short men, poor men, younger men, flops, may all have their allure to women because of—not despite—their handicaps.

It may seem amusing that I include youth as a handicap for men. What I mean is that people still regard it as a violation of the natural order of things when a woman marries a younger man. Consider all the fuss about Mary Tyler Moore's marriage at the age of forty-five to a twenty-nine-year-old doctor. If a forty-five-year-old doctor married a twenty-nine-year-old actress, would anyone give it a second thought? Our uneasy response to such matches reveals how traditional are our assumptions about power in marriage.

We don't like to talk about the element of power in relations between a man and a woman. Just the opposite. The more power is at issue, the more we tend to talk about love. Perhaps that's why marriage has always been draped in so much romantic folderol. The engagement ring, the wedding dress, the bridal showers, the honeymoon, the rhetoric of love, may all be seen as taking a woman's mind off how much she's giving up. Personally I'd welcome a moratorium on the word *love*, which blurs so many distinctions, and on romantic plots, which make it seem that the chief good or goal of a woman's life is finding a man to look up to.

The success of a modest British film called *Educating Rita* signaled that there are probably others besides me who enjoy antiromantic treatments of relations between men and women. The professor who educates Rita, enabling her to move beyond her limited life as a hairdresser, goes to Australia at the end. She does not go with him; she does not devote herself to helping him recover from alcoholism. He has helped her to have better things to do.

The fantasy of the wounded male can be seen as women's revenge against men for the disabilities imposed on them by marriage. I prefer to see it as a reflection of women's desire to be strong and to release men from the burden and responsibility of unwavering strength.

POLITICAL MURDER

Nora Astorga was a heroine of the Sandinista revolution. In 1978, when the dictator Somoza was still in power, she attracted one of his chief officials, the notoriously brutal General Reynaldo Pérez Vega, second in command of the National Guard. General Pérez pursued her and she resisted until one day she called his office and left the message that something the general was very interested in and had long been asking for could be his that day. She would be at home. When he showed up, she had him send away his bodyguards. In her bedroom, he took off his firearms. Then he was set upon and killed by Sandinista guerrillas who had been hiding there. Later Nora Astorga sent a photo of herself in guerrilla fatigues to the newspaper *La Prensa* and took full credit for her role.

In March 1984 the government of Nicaragua decided to appoint its deputy foreign minister, Nora Astorga, ambassador to the United States. The nomination was rejected by the State Department as inappropriate. Was she an accomplice to murder or a savior of her country? Was the action slaughter or revolutionary justice? We are willing to acknowledge that murder is sometimes justified by politics; otherwise, war would be impossible. But political killing off the battlefield is morally ambiguous in the extreme. On the verge of assassinating Julius Caesar, Brutus—as imagined by Shakespeare—announces that he should be seen as a "sacrificer," not a "butcher." The ambiguity remains, however. You know the figure that from one angle looks like a vase and from another a witch? Same with Brutus: from one angle a noble idealist willing to assume the terrible guilt of murder to rid his country of a tyrant; from another a self-indulgent fool who deludes himself into thinking there is an excuse for murder.

Still, however uncomfortable we are with political murder, we recognize that it exists in a different moral category from murder for personal gain or murder from passion. How you feel about it—whether you can imagine it as justified—tends to depend on two things: how long ago it happened and whether you agree with the killer's politics. The two are connected. If the assassination took place long ago, you are more willing to sympathize with the assassin's cause.

In Nora Astorga's case there was another important element: she was a woman. Political murder may be more than usually problematic when a woman is implicated. Two crimes are being committed—a murder and a betrayal of expectations about female behavior. The Bible tells the story of Jael, wife of a nomad chief, who killed the Canaanite general Sisera. After a battle in which his forces were routed by the Israelites, Sisera took shelter in the camp of Jael's husband, officially neutral but allied to the Israelites. Jael made Sisera at home in her tent, covered him with a blanket, and soothed his jangled nerves with a drink of milk. When he was asleep, she drove a wooden tent peg through his forehead. The next day she proudly acknowledged what she had done, and she is praised in the *Book of Judges* for her righteousness.

Charlotte Corday went to Paris from the provinces with the firm intention of killing Marat and thereby (she hoped) ending the Reign of Terror. She kept sending Marat requests for an appointment. He did not answer. She persevered and finally gained entry to his apartment. Marat, hearing a woman's voice, allowed her to be brought into him. Because of an illness, he had to keep his body under water, so he was in the bath when she killed him with a dinner knife bought the previous day. Charlotte Corday was tried for murder; when asked what she had to say in her defense she replied, "Nothing, except that I have succeeded." Composedly, she met her death by guillotine. She looked forward, she had said, to happiness with Brutus in the Elysian Fields.

What is strikingly similar in the stories of Charlotte Corday, the biblical Jael, and Nora Astorga is their pride in what they did and their insistence that they be given credit for their daring. All three also played on the fact that they seemed harmless to their enemies. Nora Astorga and Jael used female "hospitality" to entrap. Having disarmed her enemy by playing on notions of what a woman is like, the revolutionary heroine involved in murder defies our notions of what a woman is. She uses stereotypes of female behavior

to succeed and in succeeding overthrows the stereotypes.

Despite one's moral repugnance to any murder, the
woman who murders for a cause demands respect in
a way that Delilah, for example, that sneaky seductress,
does not. The revolutionary murderess puts her life
and her soul on the line. She fascinates because of her
daring and aggressiveness. At some level many
women, I believe, look for such stereotype-defying
heroines, even—perhaps especially—murderesses.
That is how I would explain all the interest in Jean
Harris. We wanted to see her as a heroine-murderess,
but she kept slipping out of the role into something
much smaller, and what is ultimately interesting about
the Harris case is not Mrs. Harris but the public's
response—its fascination.

If women are fascinated by female assassins for one
reason, men are fascinated for others. Women are
trained to be wary of sexual encounters, and an aggressive sexual partner is no more than most women
expect. But men—the more macho, the more innocent—go into sexual encounters assuming the harm-
lessness and passivity of their partners. That the supine
woman may rise up and turn vicious, that the adoring
mistress may become an assassin, is too terrifying to
confront.

As we know from Freud, the things we fear most
we tend to joke about. Perhaps this explains the extraordinary levity with which the American press
treated the appointment of Nora Astorga. *Time* cap-
tioned its picture of her "experienced hostess" and
ended an article on her appointment with a quotation
from a United States diplomat: "There's a limit to how
close I'd get to her." A *New York Times* editorial titled
"Femme Fatale" compared her with Marlene Dietrich

in several film roles and expressed regret that Josef von Sternberg was not around to direct her.

A woman warrior takes up an enemy general's offer to go to bed with him and helps kill him instead. To some people that's the stuff of which legends are made; to others, jokes. I, for one, wonder if a male version of Nora Astorga—a former revolutionary terrorist appointed ambassador to the United States—would be treated with such levity.

IN PRAISE OF
TOURISM

In the spring of 1984, two Americans vacationing in Sri Lanka were kidnapped by Tamil terrorists who threatened to kill them if certain conditions were not fulfilled. Tamil terrorists? Say what? How many of us when we travel understand the politics of our destinations? The horrifying spread of terrorism since 1984 has made us fitfully warier of travel but not necessarily more knowledgeable about local wars.

Some people think that Americans are getting their comeuppance for treating the world as scenic backdrop: the backdrop is sitting up and biting. With some irritation V. S. Naipaul spoke of people who thought they could buy round-trip tickets to revolutions. Robert Stone's *A Flag for Sunrise* dramatized the peculiar horror of finding yourself not exempt or invulnerable in someone else's war, and the media gave us a "true-life novel" on this theme in its coverage of the *Achille Lauro* incident and the murder of Leon Klinghoffer. In *Raiders of the Lost Ark*, there's a comic version: Indiana Jones's girlfriend flees some knife-wielding thugs in a North African bazaar, screaming, "You can't do this to me. I'm an American!"

How respectful should we be of other people's wars? The Tamils are a distinct national group within Sri Lanka, mostly Hindus who speak the language called Tamil. The majority of Sri Lankans are Buddhists who speak Singhalese. The Tamils want to carve out a separate state within Sri Lanka, Hindu in religion, Tamil in tongue. Serious stuff. But from a global perspective, Sri Lanka seems hardly big enough to split, an island the size of West Virginia.

The wars of the Tamils and the Singhalese, like all wars in which one has no stake, resemble the war between Blefescu and Lilliput in *Gulliver's Travels*, that sublime argument for the civilizing benefits of tourism, which gave us the word "lilliputian" and the concept of comic opera wars. Resisting an imperial edict that all citizens of Lilliput must open their eggs at the small end, a die-hard group determined to open their eggs at the big end fled to the nearby island of Blefescu. At the time of Gulliver's visit, the Lilliputians feared an invasion by the Big Endian rebels.

Wherever a group of people considers itself an oppressed minority—and they do so all over the globe—the potential exists for war: Catholics in Northern Ireland, Basques in Spain, Francophones in Canada, Turks in Cyprus, Tamils in Sri Lanka. An understandable nationalism splits the world into smaller and smaller bits. How far should it go? Should we sympathize with Welsh nationalism? With Cornish? Should Bequia and some other islands be allowed to secede from St. Vincent and the Grenadines, already invisible to the eye of a satellite? Does each cultural group have to have its own government in order to survive? Nationalists think so. But miniature states are like dollhouses—cute playthings. Nor does splitting seem to solve antagonisms. Hindus and Moslems continue to fight though Pakistan split off from India and Bangladesh from Pakistan. America is fortunate to have gotten this issue straight a century ago in the War of Secession: American strength has been based on size as much as on any moral superiority. We're the land of the free and the home of the big. On the other hand, where would we be if we had not won our own War of Independence? So we tend to sympathize with nationalist urges.

Margaret Zellers, author since 1979 of *Fielding's Caribbean*, was the first major guidebook author to think local politics of any concern to tourists and the first to give the subject significant space. In the last *Fielding's* before Zellers took over, Grenada was described merely as a politically autonomous member of the British Commonwealth. Vague allusions were made to "political problems," which hit tourism hard and resulted in "whimsical closings" of inns and hotels. In *Fielding's Caribbean 1984*, Zellers fully describes the revolution of 1979, which installed a socialist and pro-Cuban government in Grenada, and realistically explores the consequences for tourists of the new "socialist lifestyle": "Leave your madras jackets home." Zellers can hardly be blamed for failing to predict in the 1984 edition of her guidebook the invasion of Grenada by the United States in the fall of 1983. Readersbetween-the-lines may think she gave us fair warning by writing that Grenada "warrants the vacation time of sensitive, perceptive people."

Through jet travel we have deceptively easy physical access to places that remain closed books. One summer I went to a place I thought was Spain. I had studied Spanish to prepare myself for my visit to a friend in Barcelona. But even though I knew that my friend was an ardent Catalan nationalist, I did not really understand that the language spoken in Barcelona is Catalan, a very different kettle of fish from Spanish. My friend considers that his country, Catalunya, was taken over by foreign invaders in the sixteenth century and has been unjustly occupied ever since. Like most Barcelonans, he is bilingual in Catalan and Spanish, but he would rather speak English or French than Spanish, which he considers the language of his conquerors. It was a great joke among his friends that one of them had gotten a fellowship to teach Spanish at an American university, which had made the apparently ludicrous assumption that Spanish was her native tongue.

That you don't really know a place until you go there is a good argument for your going there and for travel being, as common wisdom has it, the best education. Travelers who expect to be greeted everywhere with open arms may be innocent, but at least, spiritually, they're on the right track. It's a toss-up as to who's more provincial, they or the terrorists who prey upon them and think they're doing something important because it's violent and makes the news. Tourism teaches us to respect local wars but encourages the aspiration of rising above them.

ON OUTSMARTING
YOURSELF

When Aeromexico flight 404 to New York from Mexico City was finally canceled at 8 P.M., I knew I would not accept the airline's offer of a nice hotel room and a place on the morning flight. That might be OK for the other three hundred people on the plane, but I was sure there was a better way.

While others accepted vouchers for rooms at the Holiday Inn and were loaded on buses, I booked myself and friend on a Mexicana flight to Chicago, leaving within an hour, with connections to New York at six in the morning. We would be home by the time the morning flight to New York left Mexico City.

In the waiting area for the Chicago flight, I saw others from flight 404 who had had the same idea: the elegant Moroccans with all the Vuitton luggage, the

Japanese businessman, the Parisian couple on their honeymoon. The entrepreneurial spirits—those who would not take no for an answer—had sorted themselves out from the mass of easygoing vacationers at Acapulco.

I have always been devoted to the Great American End Run: while everyone fights to go one way, you simply go around them. The best American End Run in which I've participated was engineered by a British friend at the end of a Bob Dylan concert in rural England in the summer of 1978. Hundreds of thousands who had made their way gradually from London to the tiny railroad stop of Blackbush in the course of the day all left at the same time, creating a backup at the train station of staggering dimensions. Hundreds of thousands stood without moving, without room for movement, for an hour at a time, until the next train bit off a piece of the crowd and the line edged up.

Panic hits me in such situations. When I stand in a crowd, waiting to be loaded, whether into vans to Holiday Inns or trains to London, some part of me fears Auschwitz. But arrogance also afflicts me. Not for me the crowds, the lines. I can figure an angle. At Blackbush we maneuvered through the woods at the side of the crowd, crossed beyond the station to the other side of town where we'd parked a car, drove in the opposite direction from London, slept the night in Gloucestershire, headed into London in the morning, and arrived, finally, by underground at the Hampstead stop, along with some sleepy, ill-shaven men who had been at the Dylan concert and had plugged on toward London throughout the night.

In Mexico, however, the end run flopped. The flight to Chicago was delayed two hours. I sat in a leather chair in an airport, fortified by Coke and coffee, listening to Keith Jarrett on my Walkman, reading a book, and feeling sorry for myself. It was 2 A.M. and I no longer cared what happened to me. When we finally boarded, we were broken with waiting. We sat down, fastened our seat belts, and heard the incredible words we had already heard once before that night: "This flight has been canceled."

I could hardly hold my boarding pass, I was so tired and hopeless. It was clear I would never get out of Mexico. "What will be will be," I decided. "Better to think like a peasant. There is nothing to be done. It is all larger than I am and out of my hands." This time only the wealthy Moroccans had the drive to get on yet another flight to Chicago. The rest of us—the Japanese businessman, the French honeymooners— finally accepted the best offer going: four hours of sleep at a hotel before the morning flight to New York.

Usually, operating on the principle that everything that can go wrong will, I like to imagine possibilities for error and forestall them. I would never dream, for example, of letting a piece of luggage move down the conveyor belt without checking where it has been ticketed to. Half the time it's on its way to some city other than the one I'm headed for. But it always turns out that there was one more error to foresee, one more thought to have, one more move to make than I could have imagined; this happens because most of the world is not as driven to outsmart itself as some of us are.

When my Honda turned four, I decided to have the clutch replaced before it actually had to be replaced. Nothing worse, I said to myself, than having the clutch fail as you're driving down the street. The car dies. You stop traffic. You have to be towed. Mess, time, waste. Get it fixed now and avoid hassles later. The day after my new clutch was installed, I suddenly lost fourth gear, then third, then second; then the car stopped in the middle of traffic. Somehow I managed to push it to the side; I called the garage and waited for the tow truck. What had happened was that when they installed my new clutch, someone had neglected to tighten the screws. They shook loose; the clutch dropped. I should have known that would happen.

It was a chastened group that boarded the Aeromexico flight from Mexico City to New York next morning. Few if any of us could take for granted many things we'd taken for granted the night before—principally, that the plane would take off and that it would land. We all clapped at touchdown, a custom that has spread rapidly in these days of ever more perilous air travel. We used to be blasé about getting where we were going. Now we see it's a miracle.

Some of us—the ones who had tried to go via Chicago—were more chastened than others. Taking another look at my fellow passengers on Aeromexico, I, highly chastened, realized they were not the tequila-addled party folks I'd originally assumed they were. One lovely woman had managed to keep a seven-month-old baby cheerful and quiet through the whole ordeal. A Mexican businessman in a cashmere coat had not a single crease more in his impeccable outfit or one hair more out of place than he'd had the night before. Whereas I, from the effort of being so smart, was a wreck.

The camaraderie of disaster brought us together and I got to know some of them. One woman lived in the town I'd grown up in. Another clucked with great sympathy when I told her of our second cancelation. She said she'd thought of trying to get on the Chicago flight but had decided against it. It was clear she felt sorry for me for having been so dumb.

LITIGATING
LITERATURE

Two recent cases brought literature to court. In one, the novelist J. D. Salinger succeeded in blocking publication of his biography. In the other, a Boston psychiatrist got the makers of the film version of *The Bell Jar* to admit that they had "unintentionally defamed" her.

These two lawsuits scare me because they so badly misunderstand literature, overvaluing the raw materials of which it is presumed to be made and undervaluing the transforming process that is art. At the bottom of both cases I see a radically mistaken metaphor for artistic activity: facts (or experience or material) plus a catalytic ingredient equals art.

Because the law is geared to protect property, and literature's complex transformations of reality fit uncomfortably into its categories, writers can be subject to sometimes comic, sometimes costly, misunderstandings in court. Fear of litigation has begun to deprive us of some of the good things of life. Is it possible that writers' fear of litigation could deprive us of literature?

In 1986 Salinger, author of *The Catcher in the Rye,* sued Random House and the biographer Ian Hamilton to halt publication of *J. D. Salinger: A Writing Life.* The book covered Salinger's creative years, the years in which, through his work, he presented himself to the public. No sensationalist exposé, it refrained from intruding into both Salinger's childhood and the twenty-three years that passed since he last published.

Salinger now is a recluse with a fanatic concern for his privacy. He rarely steps off his own land in Cornish, New Hampshire. He does not give interviews or sanction his friends' giving them about him. The lawsuit was part of his effort to keep the public from finding out anything about his life. If, however, a man is a public figure—and a writer as well known as Salinger is a public figure no matter how reclusive—he could not win a suit on the grounds of invasion of privacy.

Salinger sued instead on grounds of copyright infringement. While the law does not protect a writer's privacy, it protects his right to make money from his work. The law protects the value of Salinger's letters—even though he probably will never allow them to be published and has no intention of making money from them.

The lawsuit concerned a quantitative issue: whether Hamilton had exceeded the "fair use" standard by quoting too extensively from Salinger letters that he found in university libraries. Under the doctrine of fair use, Hamilton was allowed to quote briefly from Salinger's letters without permission and to paraphrase more, but exactly how much was a matter of judgment.

When the case went to trial, U.S. District Judge Pierre N. Leval ruled that fair use had not been exceeded, but his decision was reversed by the 2nd U.S. Circuit Court of Appeals in New York. Obviously, it was a close call on the technical grounds. But the effect of the suit—and especially of the appeals court decision banning publication of Hamilton's book—was to put biographers on guard. Like all writers, I'm concerned about maintaining copyright. But I am a biographer, and the appeals court decision seemed to discount the literary value of biography, treating it as little more than the sum of its materials and the biographer as perilously close to a thief.

On the same day Salinger won his appeal, another literary property suit was settled in Boston. A Boston psychiatrist had sued the makers of the film *The Bell Jar*, based on Sylvia Plath's novel. Dr. Jane V. Anderson sought $5 million compensation for libel and $1 million for the pain of seeing herself portrayed as a lesbian who befriends Esther Greenwood, the Sylvia Plath character, in a mental hospital, tries unsuccessfully to seduce her into a lovers' suicide pact, and eventually hangs herself. (The scene most repugnant to Anderson existed only in the film, not in the novel.)

To win her lawsuit, Anderson had to establish that she was clearly the model for the fictional character Joan Gilling. She did so by revealing that she and Sylvia Plath had grown up in the same town, gone to the same church and college, and been patients in the same mental hospital at the same time. But she denied that she had ever been a lesbian. "And certainly," as she testified straight-faced in court, "I never hung myself."

Her motives were mysterious. If, as Anderson claimed, she was pained by the invasion of her private life, why initiate a process that brought her so much dubious attention? *The Bell Jar* was a film from which people stayed away in droves. But the *Bell Jar* trial was covered daily by *The New York Times*. You might have thought she was doing it for money, but the case was settled out of court for $150,000, which may just have covered legal costs, and Anderson appeared pleased. What she wanted was vindication, and she felt she got that. Future copies of the film must carry the disclaimer that the characters are fictional and bear only coincidental resemblance to people living or dead. Of course, the film had always borne that standard disclaimer. From now on it must bear it in larger letters.

Anderson's lawyer, calling the outcome a "total victory," said that now writers stood warned to exercise "due care" in dealing with autobiographical material. But writers I know find the message confusing and scary: you shouldn't use real-life models, but if you do, you'd better be exact. Just as the Salinger case reduces biography to the materials of which it is constructed, the *Bell Jar* case reduces fiction to the "facts" on which it was "based."

People who think they've had interesting lives often believe that these constitute, potentially, books in the same way that frozen lemonade concentrate makes lemonade. Just add water and stir. Take the experiences, add time (or something called "writing ability"), and you have a novel. "Someday, if I have time, I'll write a book" is a line writers often hear—and often resent. The add-time-and-stir fallacy is related to a new, computer-generated fallacy: feed information into a computer, press "merge," and you have a book.

What writers have that other folks do not is the ability to make something out of nothing. I say "nothing" advisedly, in an attempt to destroy the notion of art as raw materials processed in time, of the artist as processor or manufacturer. An artist gets a vision of something—whether it is Hamilton's vision of Salinger's writing life or Plath's vision of her adolescence—and tries to build a model out of words, which, when read by someone else, will cause the same vision to appear in the reader's mind. Bit by bit, taking from this and that in his or her mental experience to build with, the writer brings this vision into reality, working always in the medium of words. The medium of writing is not experience. No amount of fascinating experience will ever, in itself, make a good book. Nor does any individual, no matter how eccentric, "make" a character. Nor do a bunch of quotations from letters make a biography.

Leval's lower-court decision in the Salinger case showed an understanding of literature. Defending Hamilton's use of quotations, he wrote, "It certainly tells more about Salinger to read his acid quip that anyone who has worked for 'a good upholsterer' considers himself qualified to edit a short story anthology than to be told that he resented the presumption of unqualified editors." Leval assumed that the public has a right to have an effective vision of a man they care about conveyed to them and that this conveyance depends on one effective stroke after another.

By contrast, the appeals court judges with well-intentioned myopia hovered protectively over tidbits, trying to preserve Salinger's "vividness of description" from Hamilton's appropriation. For example, in one of the letters, Salinger, furious that Oona O'Neill had ditched him for Charlie Chaplin, conjured up the couple's home life, with Chaplin "squatting grey and nude, atop the chiffonier, swinging his thyroid around his head by his bamboo cane, like a dead rat." Hamilton wrote that Chaplin, "ancient and unclothed, is brandishing his walking stick—attached to the stick, and horribly resembling a lifeless rodent, is one of Chaplin's vital organs." This hideous paraphrase, which should have been banned on literary grounds, was cited by the appeals court judges as evidence of Hamilton's using Salinger's style to enhance the value of his own book.

Because judges seem rarely to understand literature and try misguidedly to treat it as a commodity analogous to others of commercial value, we can only hope that literature stays out of court.

In sixteenth-century England, drama flourished. William Shakespeare, Christopher Marlowe, Ben Jonson—you might have thought the good plays would never stop coming. But in the seventeenth century, Puritans, who opposed drama—indeed, all literature—on the grounds that it lied, became more and more powerful. Eventually they got laws passed that forced the closing of the theaters.

These two literary lawsuits follow the Puritan tradition of noncomprehension of literature. The American courts, in the words of the English critic Christopher Hitchens, have chosen to treat "fiction as if it were biography and biography as if it were trespass." I can't imagine Americans legislating literature out of existence the way the Puritans did with English drama by flat-out prohibition. What I fear is a more indirect process: that literature will become so fraught with the peril of litigation that writers will gradually swear off it. Literature will go the way of the IUD: we will have to go to Canada to get it.

ON RECEIVING
GIFTS

W_e are told it's more
blessed to give than to receive. I disagree. To receive
is the harder task, demanding far greater resources of
tact and charity. We've all gotten gifts that would strain
the patience of a saint—the cute or perfunctory detritus
of weddings, birthday parties, weekends in the country,
Christmas, and other occasions of formal gift giving.

Because a gift represents an interpretation of our
nature, we are more likely to be irritated by a dud than
pleased, as we're supposed to be, by the thought behind
it. A gift tells us what kind of person our friends imagine us to be—wearer of clothes, grower of plants, lover
of gadgets—and we are always so much more. Gifts,
unable to address our complexity, unworthy of our
multiplicity, are potentially insulting. Books might
seem to be the answer, but they merely push the prob-

lem back a level. Which book? *The Joy of Cooking* or *The Joy of Sex?* Proust or Judith Krantz?

The messages of gifts are sometimes scary. They may say, "I am tired of the person you are. Try something new. I'm pretending that this inappropriate [fill in the blank] is a joke, but I'm really looking for someone who matches it." Other gifts say, "I've given up trying to please you. I'll just please myself, and you can take what pleasure from it you can. But I dare you to say I haven't given you anything lately." Among the more common presents intended for the donor rather than the ostensible receiver are sexy lingerie and kitchen equipment; but I recently restrained a friend, a man with a taste for fine crystal and cognac, from giving Baccarat brandy snifters to a wife who doesn't drink.

Traditional gifts are traditional for a reason: they signify less, hence risk less offense. Neutral and undemanding, flowers pay tribute to the recipient's sense of beauty. Candy is always in good taste. A tie tells a man no more than "You are a man." It is so traditional a gift as to be virtually invisible. That's the trouble with low-risk offerings: the payoff is likewise low. The gifts are bland.

Good presents speak to that elusive entity, the secret self. A hard-to-please friend recalls that the best present he ever got was a black enamel-on-gold Dumont cigarette lighter. He doesn't smoke. He doesn't know many people who smoke. He was unlikely ever to have bought himself an expensive lighter or to have received one. All the more reason he loves his. For his secret self lives in a black-and-white film of the thirties, in which an impeccably dressed man offhandedly but gracefully whips out his elegant lighter to light a friend's cigarette. Who would have known this about him, a guy who dresses in blue jeans and secondhand shirts? The secret self is touched only by indirection and luck.

Because the secret self is hard to find, gift givers belabor the self's more obvious parts. A golf player gets golf balls. A sailor gets nautical charts. Our gifts parody people: we treat women too exaggeratedly as women, and men too much as men, whereas I suspect that the secret self is often androgynous. I've never known a man or woman who didn't want a terry-cloth bathrobe. In our secret selves, we are naked, wet, emerging from the bath, longing to be wrapped up warmly.

When you consider what a perilous business this giving and receiving of gifts is, the wonder is that anyone dares it. The safest course is never to give. That way you offend no one, waste no time shopping, confer no unwelcome obligations. But from another point of view, the nongiver is a parched and meager spirit, never trying anything lest it prove the wrong thing, never offering love lest it be rejected. For what is a gift but an offer of love?

Sometimes it's an offer of love that carries with it a demand for love. You may like the present, but the fact that it has been given at all seems wrong, especially if the gift itself is overweight on the inner scale that tells you how much is appropriate. (A homemade jazz cassette is fine, but the complete Beethoven symphonies on DGG too much.) Gifts that up the stakes more quickly than the receiver would like are their own punishment. Instead of producing affection, they tend to arouse suspicion. What is wanted in return? Even if it's only gratitude, that sometimes is more than we care to give.

People who crave control find receiving gifts especially difficult. A present places them in the position of having to respond. A friend of mine says, "Please don't give me anything. I'm too hard to please. If you give me something I don't like, I hate having to act as though I like it. I don't do it well, and I resent having to do it at all."

When people have such decided tastes that nothing you give them pleases, their behavior implies, "Who are you to think you can satisfy me? Only I can please myself." The analogy with sex is inescapable. Giving pleasure and receiving it are parts of love. But some people—they make difficult friends and impossible lovers—refuse to accept pleasure. There are psycho-sexual terms to describe their behavior, but I prefer to use moral terms: they nourish a life-denying perfec-tionism. ("Only the best is good enough for me, and only I know what the best is.") This stance makes the people around them lose faith in themselves. They do worse and worse—as gift givers, as lovers. Since they know they will fail, their efforts become more and more perfunctory. If nothing pleases, why try to please? This confirms the perfectionist in her sense that she is the only capable person in a world of incompetents. Yet her clear idea of who she is is more illusory than real. A self-confident person ought to be able to wear a tacky scarf or an inappropriate bracelet without feeling her identity threatened.

I once complimented a woman on a dress she was wearing and was told it had been a gift from her hus-band. I was astonished. Did her husband know her taste so well that he could buy her clothes? She smiled and said it hadn't always been that way. When she'd got married, many years before, she'd been advised: "Accept all his gifts. For the first couple of years, you may hate them, but don't say so or you'll scare him off. He'll stop giving you things. If you're enthusiastic, he'll get better with time." And that's what this wise and happy woman did. Gift giving between any two people is like sex: if you stick with it, it gets better; and a cheerful response, over time, encourages better performance. If gifts are offers of love, they often demand the greatest act of love in return—refraining from saying exactly what you think.

One should accept gifts as a prima ballerina receives flowers at the end of a performance, without looking at them too closely but as though the tribute were one's due. One should love the world and all things in it so that every gift may be charming. Some people have this talent. They are a pleasure to give to. For the rest of us, graceful acceptance is a spiritual discipline that must be learned. Perhaps we should spend less time worrying about what to give and more learning how to receive.

OF VACATIONS

I have spent several summers on Martha's Vineyard in a converted barn with a view over the lagoon toward Vineyard Haven harbor. On the lagoon, people are shellfishing, sailing, and windsurfing. I wonder who these shellfishers, sailors, and windsurfers are. To them the holidays seem to be a time for carefree amusement. To me, and to most of the adults I know on the Vineyard, summer means cooking too much food, doing too much laundry, and making too many plans for too many people in too small a house.

A month ago—it seems forever—I was at home in Middletown, Connecticut. I had a dishwasher. I had a study, with a solid oak desk. (I write this on a bouncing card table abutting my bed.) I had privacy—doors that closed and telephones located where other people couldn't hear me talk. My son had friends to play with and ways of amusing himself that did not depend on me. I entertained occasionally but not incessantly. I worked happily all day in my study and cooked dinner from food bought at conveniently located stores. In the evening, I watched color TV and went to bed in my air-conditioned room. It was an orderly, peaceful life. When I went out, my answering machine took messages, and I returned calls.

Now I am on vacation. I pay more rent for one week in my converted barn than I pay for a month at home. Every hour is spent worrying how to amuse my son during the next one. I can't complain on the phone to my friends, because you can hear every word from all points of the converted barn. I am always washing dishes. I am always shopping and cooking and doing laundry. The floors are always sandy, and my clothes are always soggy from sea air, fog, humidity. There is a washing machine, but the spin cycle is broken. I have a string of people to entertain who would never think of coming to visit me in Middletown. I am always driving to the airport to pick them up.

If you like peace and quiet, a house in a desirable summer vacation spot is a real liability. My friend Wendy, who has a much nicer house than I do, has more visitors with expectations of better service. While her guests paddle in a canoe on the pond or wander to the barn to pat the horses, Wendy empties the dishwasher four times a day and makes three runs to town for supplies. My friend Sarah has access to a beautiful private beach. Her friends make so much use of it that one day, when the two of us wanted to talk alone, we went to a public beach for some privacy. The summer rule is, the more you have, the greater your liabilities.

E. B. White wrote a beautiful essay called "Once

More to the Lake" about the chill of mortality a man feels when he sees his son do the same summertime things he did as a child. What a luxury! E. B. White, at the lake, savors the melancholy beauty of human generations replacing one another. Meanwhile, on the beach, Wendy, Sarah, and I distribute cookies and cranberry juice, which we have remembered to purchase and to bring, and we spread the towels, which eventually we will have to launder, and we watch the next generation body surfing or playing Frisbee and in general accumulating—as we hope they will—bittersweet memories of childhood. Now don't get me wrong. I'm not opposed to nurturing. I know that many women—and even some men—positively enjoy caring for large numbers of people. I love such people and frequently take advantage of their goodness. My point is, is this a vacation?

I once had a vacation. I went to California by myself. I left my son at camp and my house and dog in the care of a kindly neighbor. I went to a Zen retreat in the mountains south of Carmel Valley. I did nothing. That is to say, I swam, sunbathed, soaked in the hot springs, and cooled off in the stream. I ate the vegetarian food provided three times a day. No menu, no choice. I did not get up at five and go to the meditation sessions. My mind was turned off, in God's own fashion, as I slept. When I left Tassajara, I went to Berkeley, where a friend, a professor, asked me what I'd read. I realized that I'd read nothing. I was mildly embarrassed. "And yet," I said, "it was a wonderful vacation." My friend, who has translated Virgil's pastoral poems and therefore knows both Latin and the theory of getting away from it all, pointed out that having read nothing and having a good vacation might be connected. The word *vacation* (he said) comes from

the Latin word *vacare,* to empty. So in the purest ety-
mological sense, a vacation is a time to empty yourself.
You empty your mind so that it can fill up again in
fresher ways. You empty yourself of attachments so
that you can return to them with enthusiasm. In whatever posture you like to do it—I prefer the classic
posture of the sunbather, facing the sun, arms slightly
out from the sides, but others may prefer sitting on a
cushion in the lotus position facing the zendo wall—
you fold in on yourself temporarily so that you can
return to the world with energy and direction. If a
vacation is an emptying, what most of us do in the
summer is not a vacation. For most of us, summer is
a filling up: more kids, more guests, more dishes, more
laundry, more plans, more things to keep track of.

Anne Morrow Lindbergh made the radical sugges-
tion in *Gift from the Sea* that a woman should go off
alone once a year if at all possible, and it may well be
that a woman can't have a real vacation with her family
around her. Much of what she needs a vacation from
is family responsibility. She needs to stop running
through the mental checklist of things to do and things
to worry about that occupies so much mental space. I
sometimes think my mind is like the surveillance cam-
era in my neighborhood grocery store, panning up and
down the aisles, keeping tabs on what goes on all over
the store, tracking the key elements of my world:
Teddy (Is he still above water? Is that sneeze a cold
or allergies? Is he happy?), the dog (Has he been fed
today? Given his heartworm pill? Walked?), the house
(Did I turn off the stove? The stereo?), the car (Where
did I leave the keys now?). On a real vacation, you
allow yourself to turn off this scanner.

Driving to the Woods Hole ferry, on the way to
Martha's Vineyard, I passed the office of a man who

called himself a "vacologist." I thought, what a lot of trouble I would save if I could stop in his office and have my mind emptied out. Of course, he was just a vacuum cleaner repairman. And, although I did not know it, I was on my way not to a vacation but to a listless career as a public servant, hotel division. Next summer, if I want a vacation, I think I'll try Manhattan. To the quiet hum of the air conditioner, perhaps I'll find peace.

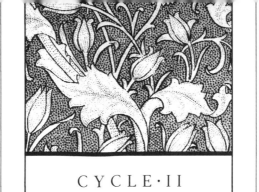

CYCLE · II

FRANCE

THE FIRST OF MAY
WITH THE MALE
WHORE OF DIJON

In France, the first of May is both Labor Day, a time for demonstrations, confrontations, and protest, and Valentine's Day, a time to celebrate friendship and love. In its latter guise, it is called the Fête des Muguets. The idea is, you give lilies of the valley (*muguets*) to people you love, and that brings them good luck for the rest of the year. On April 30, hundreds of lily-of-the-valley vendors appear on the streets. By May 1, there may be as many as a dozen people selling *muguets* at any crossroads. If you want to be authentic, you go to the woods and pick the *muguets* yourself. If you want to be extravagant, you buy them from a florist. You can wire a bunch of *muguets* from Paris to a friend in the provinces—say Besançon or Dijon—for 150 francs. On the

street a bunch costs between 8 francs and 40, $1.30 to
$6.60; in those great days a few years ago when there
were 10 francs to the dollar and I stayed in Paris for
several months doing research, 80 cents to $4.00.

On the first of May, I was in Dijon to visit Luc, a
Paris-based journalist I knew slightly who was spending a couple of weeks with his parents. I bought him
a bunch of *muguets* from an Algerian woman in the
main square of Dijon while he got some cash from the
automatic teller of the Banque Nationale de Paris. In
the back seat of his Renault, waiting to leave for a
sightseeing tour of the countryside, were two of his
Dijon friends, Denis, a homosexual prostitute, and a
transvestite also named Denis, whom I will call Denise
to avoid confusion.

Denis was conservatively dressed in blue jeans and
a black leather jacket. His hair was neatly cut, short.
He was twenty-three, and his eyes, a beautiful green,
flirted with everyone, even me. I learned as we headed
out of town that his acts of prostitution were not, by
New York standards, heavy duty. Mostly he displayed
himself, for fees ranging from 150 to 300 francs, which
is to say about $25 to $50. Occasionally he gave a
blowjob (*une pipe*) but never, for money, *une totale*. On
a good night, he got as many as three jobs, but many
nights went by with nothing at all. He had one regular
customer, a married man with a family, a teacher, who
used him two or three times a week at the highest rate,
300 francs, and liked to talk to him on the phone in
between.

Denis had the market cornered in Dijon. He was
not just another whore but *the* male whore of Dijon.
Still, it was a precarious livelihood, and he was trying
to save to start a bar.

Denise made his living as a go-go dancer. He "did

the sidewalk" occasionally, too, but not many men were interested in transvestites. Dijon was a provincial city, after all, where they were just beginning to discover pink and blue hair, black fingernail polish, and Mohawks.

It was possible to imagine a much more outrageous transvestite. His clothing was unisex rather than female: a black shirt open at the throat worn over black pants and bound by a black leather silver-studded belt, with matching dog collar around his neck. However, when he stepped daintily into the car and his pants rode up, I noticed that he shaved his legs, and he wore more makeup than I did—heavy foundation, rouge, blue pencil outlining his eyes, and black mascara. In one ear, he wore a large pearl earring, and in the other, three pearl studs in an arc. His blond hair was jelled on top to stand up and the excess tied back with a black chiffon scarf. He had on one black mesh glove without fingers. Although he was in his early twenties, he seemed to have no beard and his voice was a high falsetto. Yet Luc, who had seen him naked, assured me he was a man.

Denise wanted to be dropped off at his parents' house in Montbard, an industrial town about eighty kilometers to the northwest of Dijon, so that became the farthest point of our outing. No one was in a rush. They wanted me to see all the sights. They were proud of their native region. First, they agreed, I must taste the anise-flavored candy made by the monks at Flavigny.

It took about an hour to get to Flavigny, driving along the Burgundian canal, then into the hills. It was a walled medieval hill town, and it seemed entirely deserted. The factory store that sold the anise-flavored candy made by the local monks was closed for the first of May. So was the tobacco store. That was bad news for Denis, Denise, and Luc, who had chain-smoked Gauloises and Gitanes from Dijon to Flavigny and now were almost out of cigarettes. But it was good news for me, gagging on their smoke.

We saw no other people walking in the streets. All the more striking that against one house, a low stone-and-stucco cottage, someone had propped a ten-foot birch bough. It was freshly cut. The leaves were still green and unwithered. Luc explained this was a first of May custom. Young men leaned branches against the houses of girls they liked. You wouldn't see this in the city anymore, Luc said. You had to come out into the country to see the old customs. But what exactly the birch bough meant, whether it was an invitation, a dare, a reproach, or a compliment, Luc could not tell me.

Since nothing else was open, we wandered into the church, outsize, like all old churches, intended for larger groups than the twentieth century could provide. The boys were talking, laughing, and smoking; the old lady who guarded the place and sold postcards looked at us with disapproval. Luc, Denis, and Denise walked cursorily around the echoing stone building and left. This was not their bag. It wasn't really my bag, either, but, so as not to hurt the old lady's feelings, I stopped to buy a postcard.

"These gentlemen"—the woman said the word contemptuously—"have seen nothing of our church. They haven't thrown a glance at our angel."

"Oh," I said, "there is an angel?"

"Of course there is an angel. A very celebrated angel from the fifteenth century. And many other beautiful things in this church. But these gentlemen know nothing of them."

The church looked bereft of treasures. Nevertheless, I gave her a 3-franc tip, and she showed me the angel. It was hidden in a side chapel, a smiling Gothic angel of the Annunciation. There was also a polychrome wooden statue of the Madonna, such as Burgundy is famous for. I looked at them awhile with the woman watching me closely. Finally I thought I had looked enough. I said, "They are really beautiful. I am infinitely grateful to you for showing them to me."

"It was nothing," she replied, in the formal French phrase that sounds so rudely dismissive.

When I rejoined my pals outside, they were smoking their last cigarettes. I reported that they had irritated the caretaker by paying no attention to her angel. They were not chagrined.

"The bitch!" said Luc. "She must come from the fifteenth century herself. She has no one in her bed at night but her angel. See, Félicie, what would happen to you if you lived in a place like this? You would become old and grumpy, too."

In the car, I looked up the church at Flavigny in my guidebook. It did not mention the angel or the Madonna, merely the church's name, Saint Genest. My irony meter went berserk. Saint Genest, pronounced just like the title of Sartre's book about Genêt, and me with all these gay men. But I try to resist my own liking for irony, a cheap trick for making sense of things and then disavowing the sense you've made.

"What next, Luc?"

"Alésia, Félicie." He seemed pleased at the thought. "Do you know what happened there?"

I had no idea.

In 52 B.C. at Alésia, Julius Caesar defeated the Gauls under the gallant commander Vercingetorix. Technically a defeat ("the Waterloo of the Gauls"), this battle is a high point in French history because it marked the unification of what had been warring tribes into something resembling a nation.

Surveying the battlefield and the Burgundian hills around it is a twenty-four-foot bronze statue of Vercingetorix, with long hair and a long mustache, looking like a four-times-lifesize hippie. Around the base are the words Vercingetorix spoke to his assembled troops: "A unified Gaul, forming a single nation, animated by the same spirit, can defy the universe." At least, that is what Caesar said he said.

Caesar? Vercingetorix? A memory of alien syllables, as ineradicably part of childhood as the smell of bread when we passed the Sunshine Baking factory in Queens on the way home from Manhattan, began to come back to me: *Omnis gallia in tres partes divisa est.* Caesar didn't just fight the battle of Alésia. He wrote about it, too. And I, some nineteen hundred years later, had read his words in my high school Latin class, drilled by a buxom old maid who wore silk dresses from Lane Bryant and occasionally called me by the name of my brother, who had been her student ten years before. I was stupefied to realize that many of the ablative absolutes I had labored through had as their nominative something that had existed or happened near this very spot. The history I had read about as a girl, identifying always with Caesar and his conquering troops, had been the history of France, emerging from savagery to encounter one of the great war machines of all time. Why had I identified with the murderous Caesar when it was the Gallic hippies I loved?

Still, I couldn't resist needling Luc by pointing out that Vercingetorix's ringing words had not been true. Gaul, even unified, even animated by the same spirit—

the desire to throw the Roman bums out—had not been able to defy the world.

"He was a great man anyway. He brought the French together. When he saw we'd lost, he offered to let himself be taken prisoner if Caesar would spare the women and children. They paraded him in the streets of Rome and kept him in prison for six years and then they strangled him. I idolize him," said my cynical friend. "If he had not been what he was, we would not be what we are now."

We stood revering the twenty-four-foot bronze hippie, then rejoined Denis and Denise. They were not as moved by the site of Vercingetorix's stand against Caesar as Luc was. They thought there should be a model of the camp. Above all, they would have liked to see the houses of the camp followers. But there was only a map on which Luc showed me how far the *castrum* had extended. He began to explain what *castrum* meant, but I said he needn't bother. I knew very well the meaning of *castrum*, "camp having been pitched" and "camp having been broken" being among Caesar's absolutely favorite ablative absolutes.

"You mean you've read Caesar's *Gallic Wars*? In Latin? *Putain!*" he said.

Now literally *putain* means whore, but in this context I think it would best be translated as "Holy shit! That's unbelievable!" Luc called out to Denis and Denise, who were walking in front of us, "Hey! Listen! Can you believe this? Félicie has read Caesar's *Gallic Wars* in Latin."

Denise laughed his high girlish laugh, and Denis looked at me as though to say "I've seen lots of kinky things, but how did you get *that* idea?" As I stared back at his flirtatious eyes, I saw his point. Why had I chosen to spend my youth doing *that*?

Stunned in our various ways, we piled back into the car. We left the high battlefield and drove down a hill. At the bottom, the road ended, and before we made our turn, we found ourselves face to face with an equestrian statue of Joan of Arc. Presumably it was there, at Alésia, because Joan of Arc, too, had united the French, a feat that not only bore repeating but seemed to demand it. She was in armor, her horse was rearing back, she carried a banner, and, through the crook of her arm, someone had stuck an enormous freshly cut birch bough.

Although the Renault seemed as full of cigarette smoke as ever and I had to leave the window open to breathe, the cigarette situation, from the point of view of Luc, Denis, and Denise, was getting desperate. Just outside Alise-Sainte-Reine, the modern town of Alésia and only minimally livelier than the ancient site, we found a café that was open and sold cigarettes. Luc and I volunteered to go in.

"Get me Gitanes," Denis called after us. "Get me some ice cream. Get me a ham sandwich."

He lounged back against the window of the car, gossiping with Denise.

Inside, it was dark. Half a dozen people sat at the tables, talking and drinking wine. Behind the bar, taped on the mirror, were postcards from customers who had traveled away from this less than riveting spot: to Paris, Valenciennes, Normandy, Nice, even Alaska and Cancun. The postcard from Alaska showed a dog sled crossing the snow. The one from Cancun showed a barebreasted woman, on the sand in front of a hotel, holding high a beach ball.

We bought the cigarettes and a sandwich for Denis. Back at the car, Denise repaid Luc for his cigarettes, but Denis said he had no money.

"OK," said Luc. "That's three *pipes* and a *totale* you owe me."

Now they wanted to take me to Fontenay Abbey, a Cistercian monastery built on the edge of the Fontenay Forest because that seemed like the end of the world in 1118. Bernard of Clairvaux had wanted to get as far as possible from the distractions of city life in order to live deliberately. For centuries it worked. Only in the sixteenth century did the abbey start going downhill, and during the Revolution it became a paper mill. Now it has been beautifully restored and opened to tourists.

Since Fontenay is close to his hometown, Denise had already seen it. He didn't come inside with us but waited by the car, smoking. Denis, too, was reluctant to come in. He hadn't seen the place, but there was a steep admission charge of 26 francs. I offered to pay for him. He accepted. I got a kick out of paying for a whore, even if it was just to see a medieval cloister. To tell the truth, I should say it was a kick to pay for a whore especially to see a medieval cloister; such are the seductions of irony.

Because the Cistercians were opposed to ornament, the buildings were austere. The monks slept in a common dormitory off the church.

"What a good idea!" said Denis.

"They slept on straw mats on the floor," I reminded him.

"They had to huddle together to keep warm," he countered.

"Even huddling, they must have frozen," said Luc, looking up at the ceiling sixty feet above us. The roof beams were from the fifteenth century, hand-carved Spanish chestnut, intricately crisscrossed.

"*Quelle putain de charpente!*" said Luc—literally,

"What a whore of a ceiling," or, as I would have translated it, "Those are some fucking roof beams!"

In the church, there was a Gothic sculpture of the Madonna and Child. "*Quelle putain de statue!*" said the appreciative Luc.

Near the forge, where the monks made tools, the stream used for power had been stepped down and softened into a pond and stocked with fat trout. "*Putain!*"

We dropped Denise off at his parents' house, one in a row of identical, low, attached factory workers' houses such as you see in 1950s British films about the Midlands. Young D. H. Lawrence might have grown up in such a house, on such a treeless, charmless street.

Denise carried no books in a book bag or clothes in a suitcase. He walked into the house without waiting or knocking: the door was unlocked. What would he find there? How did his family feel about a son who wore blue eye liner, a pearl in his ear, a chiffon scarf on his hair, a dog collar around his neck, and one mesh glove with no fingers? We wondered, too, Luc and I, what he would do there for the next two weeks. Watch TV? There wasn't much on during the day. This wasn't America. Luc and I could not imagine Denise's life in Montbard. But Denis was indignant on his behalf.

"One has pals, after all. What do you think he is?"

Well, there you are. "One has pals." I was embarrassed, for Denis had understood me perfectly. I had assumed Denise was a freak. But even a transvestite go-go dancer in a factory town in the provinces has friends. How had I come to be in this company if not through the human propensity to filament?

My friend David, on vacation in Rio, noticed from the window of his hotel a cute guy in a hotel across the way. They met at the airport. They were on the same charter flight back to New York. Luc had seen David looking at him from the hotel across the way, and he thought David was cute, too. He was working in New York for a year. He was lonely. His English wasn't that good. He and David tried sex and became friends.

Back in France, Luc was too broke one year to travel during his vacation. He had to stay with his parents in Dijon if he was going to get out of Paris at all. He expected to die of boredom. Instead, one night in a café he met Denis, who cruised him. Luc had no money for sex, so they became friends. Through Denis he met Denise and what he called "an amusing group of young people in Dijon."

Now I enter the picture. When I first got to Paris, I was homesick and lonely. I wrote a sad letter to David, and he wrote a letter to Luc. For David's sake, Luc was nice to me. He took me through Père Lachaise by motor bike; we went drinking in trendy places around Les Halles. When he invited me to visit him at his parents' home in Dijon, I went and so met Denis and Denise.

What strikes me, looking back, is just how comfy a foursome we made that day—united against boredom, against loneliness, against eventual obliteration, against the indifference of history. As Vercingetorix might have said, even a journalist, a transvestite, a whore, and a visiting American, animated by the same spirit, can defy the universe.

GRAFFITI
IN THE CAVE
OF THE MAMMOTHS

I visited the cave of Rouffignac on a day of sun showers, but inside it was cold and dark. Rouffignac is what they call a dry cave, which means that it was formed by water moving laterally from a central well, not by seepage from the surface. Thus, it has no stalactites, and the walls are relatively smooth. Red stones projecting from the walls are broken off where bears sharpened their claws. Craters in the stone floor were scooped out by bears for their winter-long snoozes. Fifteen thousand years ago, men and bears competed for living space in these caverns of the soft stone cliffs along the Dordogne and Vézère rivers.

Now an electric train carries you two miles into the cliff to see the wall paintings. Whoever drew the figures walked that distance to make those drawings in that spot. He drew three rhinoceros walking in a line. Farther on, someone engraved a figure into the soft stone. The guide's flashlight follows the outline of the tusks, the trunk, the rounded skull, the downward curve connecting skull to hump: a mammoth, suggested with eloquent simplicity. Farther on, in a great hall, there are more than sixty figures of animals. On the ceiling is a horse so large that whoever painted it could not have seen the whole at once. He had to visualize the proportions. But there are other sophisticated feats. For one, a frieze of mammoths, two herds of them, coming together nose to nose in the center of a wall. In one herd, a straggler walks a few paces behind the others. Someone composed these images for this space. Someone had an idea on a grand scale and executed it.

"If we talk about 'prehistoric art,' we give it an illusory unity," said the guide. "Really, there are just flashes. A couple of generations of artists at one time in one place, passing down their skills from father to son. Somehow the line is broken. Then it's over for that locale. Rouffignac and Lascaux are close in kilometers. You might imagine there was a kind of art school around here. But they are separated by four thousand years. A hundred years perhaps of genius at each place with thousands of years in between. Flashes."

It is but a step from this talk of "flashes" of creativity to talk of "the human spirit." I feel it coming in myself. I am moved by these drawings, by the idea of a man walking two miles into the earth to make them, by the idea of a craft being handed down from father to son for some hundred years eleven thousand years ago. I don't know how to identify the source of my emotion except by that phrase so useful to sentimental humanists like me, "the human spirit." I remind myself how lopsided it would be to see "the human spirit" at Rouffignac just in the glorious drawings of the mammoths, horses, and mountain goats. The human spirit is there even more abundantly in the graffiti that cover the walls and ceilings and come close to effacing some prehistoric drawings. Enormous, dark, graceless, unignorable, "BOUTIER 1906" is inscribed right across a beautiful bison from 9000 B.C.

The human spirit is impelled to register its triumphs. When it walks two miles into the earth and finds something interesting, it wants to say "I got here. I count for something. I can't draw a mammoth perhaps, but I can write my name." Poet-graffitist Lord Byron carved his name on a Greek temple. The urges toward creation and destruction are not so separable as we might like. Boutier is the human spirit saying, "I destroy, therefore I am."

Defaced as it is by graffiti, the cave of Rouffignac has been visited continuously since the sixteenth century. The history of nearby Lascaux is very different. It was discovered only in 1940, when four boys in search of a lost dog found the frescoed chamber that has been called "the Sistine Chapel of prehistory." In 1963 it was closed to the public. The discovery of the frescoes had initiated their destruction. Exposure to the outside air and the breath of visitors stimulated the growth of green algae and then a white calcite covering that, even now, unseen, continue to obliterate the paintings.

Sometimes the opposite happens: the past takes revenge on the present. One should be careful about opening caves. When King Tut's tomb, unviolated since 1350 B.C., was opened in 1922, two dozen of the tomb's explorers died premature, mysterious deaths. It was called "the curse of the Pharaoh," and the way it worked has recently been explained by a French physician. Fruits and vegetables left for the Pharaoh to eat in eternity decayed in time, producing a toxic mold. Severe allergic reaction to that mold caused the explorers to die from pulmonary insufficiency, strangled by the past.

Time may be kind or cruel, but, like nature, it is morally neutral. Man stops time by certain gestures: a mammoth drawn in magnesium bioxide on a cave wall in the Dordogne, a scrawled signature "BOUTIER 1906" painted over it. Some things are better than others and deserve to endure. That doesn't mean they will.

They built a reproduction of the Lascaux cave. It took ten years to build. It is so faithful, they say only an archaeologist can tell the difference between it and the original. But of course there is one big difference: the original is decaying and the copy never will. I find I cannot work up much enthusiasm for Lascaux II, not enough to wait in the long line for tickets. I go to these caves only partly to see the shapes and outlines of beauty. Books and postcards show me that. Mostly I go to feel the chill I get in the actual presence of beauty that has survived the neutral menace of nature and the active malice of man. Primitively, atavistically, magically, I go to partake of art's strength. Perhaps, in his misguided way, that's what Boutier wanted, too—to shelter his miserable transience against the rock drawing's enduring power.

TOOLS OF TORTURE

In a gallery off the rue Dauphine, near the *parfumerie* where I get my massage, I happened upon an exhibit of medieval torture instruments. It made me think that pain must be as great a challenge to the human imagination as pleasure. Otherwise, there's no accounting for the number of torture instruments. One would be quite enough. The simple pincer, let's say, which rips out flesh. Or the head crusher, which breaks first your tooth sockets, then your skull. But in addition I saw tongs, thumbscrews, a rack, a ladder, ropes and pulleys, a grill, a garrote, a Spanish horse, a Judas cradle, an iron maiden, a cage, a gag, a strappado, a stretching table, a saw, a wheel, a twisting stork, an inquisitor's chair, a breast breaker, and a scourge. You don't need complicated machinery to cause incredible pain. If you want to saw your victim down the middle, for example, all you need is a slightly bigger than usual saw. If you hold the victim upside down so that the blood stays in his head, hold his legs apart, and start sawing at the groin, you can get as far as the navel before he loses consciousness.

Even in the Middle Ages, before electricity, there were many things you could do to torment a person. You could tie him up in an iron belt that held the arms and legs up to the chest and left no point of rest, so that all his muscles went into spasm within minutes and he was driven mad within hours. This was the twisting stork, a benign-looking object. You could stretch him out backward over a thin piece of wood so that his whole body weight rested on his spine, which pressed against the sharp wood. Then you could stop up his nostrils and force water into his stomach through his mouth. Then, if you wanted to finish him off, you and your helper could jump on his stomach, causing internal hemorrhage. This torture was called the rack. If you wanted to burn someone to death without hearing him scream, you could use a tongue lock, a metal rod between the jaw and collarbone that prevented him from opening his mouth. You could put a person in a chair with spikes on the seat and arms, tie him down against the spikes, and beat him, so that every time he flinched from the beating he drove his own flesh deeper onto the spikes. This was the inquisitor's chair. If you wanted to make it worse, you could heat the spikes. You could suspend a person over a pointed wooden pyramid and whenever he started to fall asleep, you could drop him onto the point. If you were Ippolito Marsili, the inventor of this torture, known as the Judas cradle, you could tell yourself you had invented something humane, a torture that worked without burning flesh or breaking bones. For the torture here was supposed to be sleep deprivation.

The secret of torture, like the secret of French cuisine, is that nothing is unthinkable. The human body is like a foodstuff, to be grilled, pounded, filleted. Every opening exists to be stuffed, all flesh to be carved off the bone. You take an ordinary wheel, a heavy wooden wheel with spokes. You lay the victim on the ground with blocks of wood at strategic points under his shoulders, legs, and arms. You use the wheel to break every bone in his body. Next, you tie his body onto the wheel. With all its bones broken, it will be pliable. However, the victim will not be dead. If you want to kill him, you hoist the wheel aloft on the end of a pole and leave him to starve. Who would have thought to do this with a man and a wheel? But, then, who would have thought to take the disgusting snail, force it to render its ooze, stuff it in its own shell with garlic butter, bake it, and eat it?

Not long ago I had a facial—only in part because I thought I needed one. It was research into the nature and function of pleasure. In a dark booth at the back of the beauty salon, the aesthetician put me on a table and applied a series of ointments to my face, some cool, some warmed. After a while she put something into my hand, cold and metallic. "Don't be afraid, madame," she said. "It is an electrode. It will not hurt you. The other end is attached to two metal cylinders, which I roll over your face. They break down the electricity barrier on your skin and allow the moisturizers to penetrate deeply." I didn't believe this hocus-pocus. I didn't believe in the electricity barrier or in the ability of these rollers to break it down. But it all felt very good. The cold metal on my face was a pleasant change from the soft warmth of the aesthetician's fingers. Still, since Algeria it's hard to hear the word *electrode* without fear. So when she left me for a few minutes with a moist, refreshing cheesecloth over my face, I thought, "What if the goal of her expertise were pain, not moisture? What if the electrodes were electrodes in the Algerian sense? What if the cheesecloth mask were dipped in acid?"

In Paris, where the body is so pampered, torture seems particularly sinister, not because it's hard to understand but because—as the dark side of sensuality—it seems so easy. Beauty care is among the glories of Paris. *Soins esthétiques* include makeup, facials, massages (both relaxing and reducing), depilations (partial and complete), manicures, pedicures, and tanning, in addition to the usual run of *soins* for the hair: cutting, brushing, setting, waving, styling, blowing, coloring, and streaking. In Paris the state of your skin, hair, and nerves is taken seriously, and there is little of the puritanical thinking that tries to persuade us that beauty comes from within. Nor do the French think, as Americans do, that beauty should be offhand and low maintenance. Spending time and money on *soins esthétiques* is appropriate and necessary, not self-indulgent. Should that loving attention to the body turn malevolent, you have torture. You have the procedure—the aesthetic, as it were—of torture, the explanation for the rich diversity of torture instruments, but you do not have the cause.

Historically, torture has been a tool of legal systems, used to get information needed for a trial or, more directly, to determine guilt or innocence. In the Middle Ages confession was considered the best of all proofs, and torture was the way to produce a confession. In other words, torture didn't come into existence to give vent to human sadism. It is not always private and perverse but sometimes social and institutional, vetted by the government and, of course, the church. (There have been few bigger fans of torture than Christianity and Islam.) Righteousness, as much as viciousness, produces torture. There aren't squads of sadists beating down the doors to the torture chambers, begging for jobs. Rather, as a recent book on torture by Edward Peters says, the institution of torture creates sadists; the weight of a culture, Peters suggests, is necessary to recruit torturers. You have to convince people that they are working for a great goal in order to get them to overcome their repugnance to the task of causing physical pain to another person. Usually the great goal is the preservation of society, and the victim is presented to the torturer as being in some way out to destroy it.

From another point of view, what's horrifying is how easily you can convince someone that he is working for the common good. Perhaps the most appalling psychological experiment of modern times, by Stanley Milgram, showed that ordinary, decent people in New Haven, Connecticut, could be brought to the point of inflicting (as they thought) severe electric shocks on other people in obedience to an authority and in pursuit of a goal, the advancement of knowledge, of which they approved. Milgram used—some would say abused—the prestige of science and the university to make his point, but his point is chilling nonetheless. We can cluck over torture, but the evidence at least suggests that with intelligent handling most of us could be brought to do it ourselves.

In the Middle Ages, Milgram's experiment would have had no point. It would have shocked no one that people were capable of cruelty in the interest of something they believed in. That was as it should be. Only recently in the history of human thought has the avoidance of cruelty moved to the forefront of ethics. "Putting cruelty first," as Judith Shklar says in *Ordinary Vices*, is comparatively new. The belief that the "pursuit of happiness" is one of man's inalienable rights, the idea that "cruel and unusual punishment" is an evil in itself, the Benthamite notion that behavior should be guided by what will produce the greatest happiness for the greatest number—all these principles are only two centuries old. They were born with the eighteenth-century democratic revolutions. And in two hundred years they have not been universally accepted. Wherever people believe strongly in some cause, they will justify torture—not just the Nazis, but the French in Algeria.

Many people who wouldn't hurt a fly have annexed to fashion the imagery of torture—the thongs and spikes and metal studs—hence reducing it to the frivolous and transitory. Because torture has been in the mainstream and not on the margins of history, nothing could be healthier. For torture to be merely kinky would be a big advance. Exhibitions like the one I saw in Paris, which presented itself as educational, may be guilty of pandering to the tastes they deplore. Solemnity may be the wrong tone. If taking one's goals too seriously is the danger, the best discouragement of torture may be a radical hedonism that denies that any goal is worth the means, that refuses to allow the nobly abstract to seduce us from the sweetness of the concrete. Give people a good croissant and a good cup of coffee in the morning. Give them an occasional facial and a plate of escargots. Marie Antoinette picked a bad moment to say "Let them eat cake," but I've often thought she was on the right track.

All of which brings me back to Paris, for Paris exists in the imagination of much of the world as the capital of pleasure—of fun, food, art, folly, seduction, gallantry, and beauty. Paris is civilization's reminder to itself that nothing leads you less wrong than your awareness of your own pleasure and a genial desire to spread it around. In that sense the myth of Paris constitutes a moral touchstone, standing for the selfish frivolity that helps keep priorities straight.

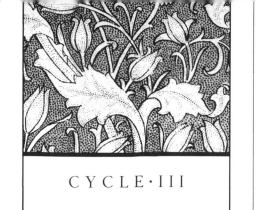

CYCLE·III

NEW
ENGLAND

NEVER SAY
GOODBYE

Two miles outside Higganum, Connecticut, on rural Route 81, is a store named Never Say Goodbye. To call it an antique shop would give the wrong impression entirely. There is some furniture for sale, but furniture is not the store's strength. Hanging from the ceiling, hanging over doors, hanging on racks, are old dresses, trousers, blouses, nightgowns, capes, stoles, bathrobes, furs. There are racks of shoes, racks of hats, cases of jewelry, tables full of handbags, fur muffs, sheet music, vases, tableware, tablecloths, and lace. What makes the place extraordinary is not so much the variety as the depth in any area. A whole section is devoted to wedding dresses, another to tuxedoes, another to bed jackets. The alligator shoes alone would fill a closet. Hats frame two doorways and spill over to a bookcase; lace collars are tacked on a wall in rows. Each section constitutes a collection. There is so much of everything that one feels in the presence of a passion rather than a cool and reasoned attempt to sell.

I, for one, share the passion. I go to Never Say Goodbye to try on—and sometimes buy—vintage clothing. My favorites are chiffon dresses of the 1920s, but I also like 1920s lace and crêpe de Chine from the 1930s. Some days, trying on flowered peach chiffon, I'm Zelda Fitzgerald, spoiled, talented, doomed. Other days, in navy blue crêpe, I'm Eleanor Roosevelt, elegantly dowdy, doing good. It's like being let loose in a film company's costume department. The store is a playland for grownups, and shopping there is a way of giving rein to fantasies that adult life usually inhibits.

My sister finds distasteful the idea of having against her skin clothes that someone else has worn. She would no more put on a chiffon beaded dress that an unknown woman bought at an unknown store in the twenties than she would wear her neighbor's underwear. This difference between us could be attributed to the fact that she is older than I am and did not have the training I did in wearing hand-me-downs. But I prefer to think it's because she has spent her adult life in New York, whereas I have spent mine in New England. She looks to the new for value; I look to the old.

Sifting the past for value is a New England obsession, pursued in colleges and universities but equally at tag sales, antiques fairs, and junk shops (never called that), which seem to be more profuse here than in other parts of the country.

The first thing one learns from this exercise is how relative value is. One summer day, at a tag sale held by the United Methodist Ladies of Oak Bluffs on Martha's Vineyard, just outside the nineteenth-century gingerbread enclave on the meeting grounds, I spotted a gold candelabra I had to have. It held three candles and was covered in gilded roses. I made myself put a figure to how much I wanted it before I started bargaining. I decided I would pay $5.00 happily and would even go up to $8.00. But when I asked the frail, white-haired lady behind the table how much she was asking for the piece, she said, "Ten." I was surprised. I thought that was high. "Can you do any better?" I asked. It was her turn to look surprised. "Better than ten cents?"

One dreams of the opposite—finding certified treasure amid dross, the East Coast version of prospecting. A friend and I attended a tag sale at the Connecticut Valley home of some people who had belonged to a print club in the 1930s. Their heirs were selling their collection at a dollar a print. My friend bought a Segonzac, which he took to a dealer the next day and sold for $200. His purchase, which ensured that something wonderful would not be thrown out with the garbage, was as much an act of conservation as of acquisition. The day my friend found his Segonzac, I found a Martin Lewis, which I won't sell until I'm in the Home for the Aged and need the money for medicine. Whenever I make another bad investment on the stock market, I console myself by thinking of my great investments in "junk."

It seems to me typical of New England to think that good things will only get better in time, that in fact time is necessary to prove whether they are good. Remember that once-hallowed concept "the test of time"? I do not feel alone here believing in it. I have an image of time battering against an object to reveal its essential quality, as vivid as that of a solution, to which a precipitate has been added, turning green to indicate copper. A New York editor once described some of my work, disparagingly, as "timeless." She encouraged me to write something "timely" for a change. But I was educated in New England. For me, "timeless" is the highest praise there is.

There are Bostonians, I know, who do not consider Connecticut part of New England, but it is, very much so. This is proved by the fact that a Connecticut governor, the late, beloved Ella Grasso, held a tag sale when she wanted to clear out her house. Both buyers and sellers at tag sales are demonstrating another trait I associate with New England—thrift. This is not to be confused with bargain hunting. The bargain hunter takes a taxi from one side of New York to the other to save a few dollars at a stocking sale or buys a fur coat that she doesn't really want simply because it's a good buy. Far different the practitioner of thrift! She may replace her electric juicer with an old-fashioned kind because she prefers its feel, but she will be sure to sell the electric one at her next tag sale. She will wear a tag sale belt with expensive clothes if the belt holds up her pants as she wants them held.

I use as my typing table a hospital table, the kind they place over beds for food trays. Mine is wood and hence outmoded. I bought it for a dollar and, lapped over my desk, it supports a typewriter perfectly. I consider that thrift. Hanging on my walls and lying on my floors are quilts and rugs I bought during many summers in different parts of New England when I was finished working for the day and wanted something else to do. On my bed is a rag rug I bought at an antiques fair in Deerfield, Massachusetts. The colors are still good, the rug still covers. It was cheaper than a custom bedspread. That, too, is thrift.

I no longer buy quilts. They have been discovered. Even at tag sales, their prices are high. The same thing has happened to photographs—visiting cards, stereopticon cards, tintypes, daguerrotypes, which the careful shopper used to be able to pick up for virtually nothing. People have caught on. It requires intelligence and a bit of prescience to stay ahead of the crowd, to figure out what is undervalued and to buy it while one can still afford it. Now I buy rag rugs and vintage clothes.

Sometimes I get tired, staying ahead of the game like that. I wish I could walk into a store on Newbury Street or Madison Avenue and extravagantly buy, let us say, a fur coat or an oriental rug or designer clothes without putting in all the time that's necessary to do things the thrifty way. But then I remind myself of something I've believed for a long time that is the playful side of thrift: anyone can live well on lots of money. The trick is to do it on little.

I take people I love to Never Say Goodbye, but not all of them see its charm. My mother said, "The lighting is terrible. How do they expect you to see the goods?" It's true. The lighting is warm and atmospheric but on the dark side. There are so many dresses squeezed together on a rack that to see any one dress involves exerting major force to push aside the others. Never mind that on the fall day I was there with my mother, a pot of mulled cider scented the store and browsers were invited to help themselves. That doesn't help one see "the goods." My mother, you see, is a New Yorker. Her idea of a good store is Bloomingdale's, Bergdorf's, or Bendel's.

SEAMUS IN LOVE

I have an English springer spaniel named Seamus (pronounced like *shameless* without the *l*). One day as I was walking him across the college campus on which I live, a young woman approached me with a proposition. She had a female springer. Would I be interested in breeding my dog with hers? "Sure," I said, "why not?"

As the time of Britannia's heat neared, her owner, Penny, asked if she could take Seamus walking with Britannia. It was her idea that the dogs should "get to know one another." Thus Seamus and Britannia began to date. Sometimes they went to the park and sometimes to the cemetery. Sometimes I went along. Penny showed me places in the old cemetery where wild-flowers grow. The dogs seemed to like romping together.

I confess I was skeptical from the beginning about Penny's plan for the dogs to be friends. Bad enough to think that humans have to be friends before they are lovers. More irrelevant yet for dogs. Friendship takes a long time; sex doesn't.

Irises and poppies bloomed in the cemetery. Seamus started running away in search of Britannia. Never before had I needed to tie him up. He had always stayed near my house. Now he roamed. My name and phone number were on a tag on his collar. People would phone me from all over town and say they had my dog. Would I come get him? I would be cooking dinner, working, or getting ready for bed; a call would come about Seamus. Off I'd go in my car to pick him up. Inside the house he made so much noise that even if I banished him from my study, I could hear him downstairs, moaning. I began to wish I'd never introduced him to Britannia. If I hadn't thrust sex upon him, would he have discovered it?

One day the dog warden nabbed him, so I had to drive even farther than usual and pay a $10 fine to reclaim him. The warden chastised me mildly for allowing Seamus to roam, and I couldn't help pouring out my heart: "I can't control him anymore. He slips away whenever I open the door. He has a girlfriend—spring fever. It's driving me crazy. Will it get any better afterward?" For Britannia was still not in heat.

I hoped my problems would be solved when Britannia went into heat. Then we could return to placid normality. But as Britannia approached the time and Seamus's interest became more obsessive, Britannia made it clear that she considered Seamus only a friend. In the woods, in the cemetery, when he tried to approach her, she bit him or ran away.

Britannia had a thing for German shepherds, or, at

least, she had once allowed herself a rendezvous in a dark parking lot with a semimongrel German shepherd. Drawn to mysterious, déclassé, and somewhat brutal strangers, Britannia felt no pull to cute little Seamus (a "preppie dog," someone once said), so appropriate for her, so much the right sort—and perhaps for that reason erotically uninteresting.

Penny's anthropomorphic scheme had failed. Letting the dogs "get to know one another" had not produced sexual attraction. But Penny still wanted puppies, so we took the dogs to the vet for help.

I will spare you the details of what exactly happened so that Seamus and Britannia might genetically combine, but I will say that the dogs were in no contact of any sort, while Seamus and the vet were intimately connected. Four women—Penny, two nurses, and I—watched the vet at work with Seamus. When Seamus suddenly looked stunned, we, the female spectators, spontaneously cheered. The transfer was effected by syringe and the business was completed. Penny was disappointed. "It's so clinical," she said. But it didn't seem clinical to me. It seemed human in the best sense of the word: using ingenuity to make the best of a bad situation, seizing on whatever spin-offs of satisfaction might be produced. Human, a little kinky, but not clinical, though certainly not romantic.

Britannia did not conceive—appropriately, since nothing else in this romance went the way Penny wanted it to do. She seemed to think the dogs should have dated, fallen in love, gotten engaged and married, and, with deep affection and commitment, made love. Of this lovemaking puppies would have come.

Perhaps I should not mock Penny's attitude. The sentimentalization of sex is one of civilization's highest and most complex achievements, taking centuries to accomplish. I know I should respect this advance. But Seamus in the throes of love seemed—well—like an animal. The sentimentalization of sex is an achievement, all right, but a dubious one.

Freud pointed out how our contemporary attitude to love differs from that of the ancients: the ancients revered the instinct, whereas we glorify its object. To the ancients love was a force, a power, a goddess who impelled one helter-skelter after various goals. A wise person respected and tried to placate this force, as one would respect the power of the sea, the wind, or any other force of nature. Greek literature is filled with characters who, showing insufficient respect for Aphrodite, are punished for it. Hippolytus, a high-minded youth, prides himself on his chastity. Aphrodite rebukes him for his presumption by making his stepmother, Phaedra, lust for him. It all ends badly.

Our way is different. We tend to justify passion by justifying our love objects: Christopher, George, or Jerry is uniquely worthy of our love. We like to believe our feeling is a reasonable response to an external provocation—the excellence of Christopher, Jerry, or George. We prefer to disregard the extent to which our spontaneous and perhaps ludicrous love has irradiated and transformed Christopher or Jerry. Sometimes when I discuss Shakespeare with undergraduates, they tell me that all the trouble occurred between Othello and Desdemona because they did not take time to get to know each other. "She loved me for the dangers I had passed / And I loved her that she did pity them" does not seem to many students a good basis for a "solid relationship." Romeo and Juliet seem pretty precipitate, too.

Passion being irrational, its effects are often ridiculous, which we do not like to acknowledge. The second act of Balanchine's ballet *A Midsummer Night's Dream* contains a pas de deux intended to express the abstract, essential nature of love. But the first act, staying closer to Shakespeare, presents a tableau of Titania and Bottom: the beautiful queen of the fairies strokes the head of the workman turned ass, crowns him with flowers, tells him how wonderful he is. That, not the pas de deux, seems to me the abstract, essential image of love.

And what of our lovers, Seamus and Britannia? Seamus got over it. Like a fever, lovesickness peaks and breaks. He recovered partly after the mating at the vet's. When he lay on my study floor after that, he no longer whimpered. He dreamed peacefully, though whether of Britannia or the veterinarian I do not know. Penny moved to Massachusetts, taking Britannia with her. She left Seamus a present—a sock Britannia had played with—to remember his girlfriend by. I threw the sock away. I thought he was better off forgetting her.

SELF-ESTEEM,
SELF-DISGUST

One day a young man presented a bouquet to Janice, the secretary of the English Department. She was astounded. "But I don't even know you!" she said. He quickly explained that he was just the florist's messenger; the card would tell her who had sent the flowers. They came, as it happened, from a grateful professor for whom she had done some work. But what strikes me is that for a split second she thought a complete stranger was offering her flowers, and although this surprised her, it was not inconceivable.

Why should it be? Don't we all harbor fantasies of a brass band's arriving at our door to play in our honor? Of Warren Beatty's standing on our front step with a red ribbon around his neck? I know I do. Like gold coins in a garbage dump, sprinkled here and there in the midst of our self-distrust are these glittering visions of our worth and importance. We may suspect during many waking hours that we have no worth or importance and at the same time hope that the world, perhaps in the form of a young man bearing flowers, will one day pay them tribute.

Such fantasies seem to me entirely healthy, as bankable as my metaphorical gold coins. Sometimes they are linked to myths we hold about our lives. Everyone, for example, has a story about his or her birth. I was born in Doctors Hospital with the fleet massing in the East River beneath my mother's window for the invasion of North Africa. Was the fleet really massing in the East River for the invasion of North Africa? An easy question to answer for certain, but I never will, for the facts in this case, as in many others, are less important to me than their significance, the myth.

Some part of me thinks—has always thought—that the invasion of North Africa was an elegant pretext, a cover story, an excuse. World War II or no, the fleet would have been there festively "massing"—I imagine this to consist of a lot of nuzzling between ships and blowing of horns—in honor of my birth. The fleet massed for me the way the fairies gathered for the birth of Sleeping Beauty. The fleet bestowed blessings on me and wished me well in life. On successive birthdays I have waited for the fleet, in some form, to return. It never does. Nevertheless, whatever is strong in my ego may be said to be strong because I believe that the fleet massed below my mother's window on the day of my birth.

The expectation that the world will congratulate us for living tends to focus on birthdays, and usually what happens on birthdays is nothing. I'm speaking of adults. Indeed, that's one way you can tell when you've grown up: nothing happens on your birthday. I knew I was grown up when I turned thirty-eight and even my mother forgot my birthday. I was so depressed after looking through the mail that I went back to bed. My son, then eight, found me there, the shades drawn on a bright Saturday afternoon. I disclosed the problem. "Don't move," he said. "I'll be right back." Half an hour later he returned and thrust something large at me in a brown paper bag. "You don't have to use these," he said, "but I want you to have them." He had grabbed all his capital—$2.00—and gone to the nearest store and bought the biggest thing he could get for his money: a five-pound bag of potatoes. Now I have a special place in my heart for potatoes. Still, it's not the fleet or a brass band or Warren Beatty.

The average person's mixture of arrogance and self-loathing, of daring and fear, never ceases to amaze me. We want to bring down the house. We want the house to stand, protecting us. We want to be invulnerable through strength. We want to be invulnerable because there's nothing there to hurt. We want to be everything and nothing. I sometimes believe I am the prize package my kindly parents always told me I was. But just as often, getting out of bed in the morning seems a plucky thing to do. (At such moments of existential panic, I find enormously helpful the phrase "another day, another dollar," which takes the risky business of getting out of bed away from metaphysics and into the realm of the practical, where it belongs.)

Often I think I'm the only person for the job, whatever the job may be: cooking pasta al pesto, planning a trip, writing a certain biography. But often I feel like an impostor as a writer, teacher, human being. I like attention but I suffer from stage fright. If I had to say what it is I'm afraid of, I guess it's that my self won't be there when I need it. I'm afraid people will see through me and find there's nothing there.

I once appeared on a TV talk show with Joey Skaggs, the artist who specializes in putting things over on people. For example, he will announce that he intends to windsurf from Hawaii to California or that, as king of the Gypsies, he is calling for a work stoppage of Gypsies to protest the term *gypsy moth*. People believe him, and that constitutes the work of art. He is a media artist, a public relations artist. I like his work and envy his talent. Before the TV show, we chatted. He showed me his clippings, an enormous scrapbook full of them. Worried that I would be found invisible when I appeared on TV, I could not bring myself to look at this massive evidence of Joey Skaggs's reality. I guess he thought I was bored by it or contemptuous. "It's hard to take in all at once," he said. I told him that wasn't the problem. "It makes me feel like nothing by comparison," I said. Joey, a nice man, conned me into comfort. "Believe me," he said, waving his hand to take in the studio and his clipping book, "it's all this that's nothing."

I used to think these problems of self-esteem were peculiarly female. Now I'm not sure. When I began teaching fourteen years ago, I was convinced that establishing authority in the classroom was more of a problem for me than for my male colleagues. Before the start of each semester I had terrible anxiety dreams: I would go to composition class prepared to teach Shakespeare or vice versa, I would suddenly be called upon to lecture on the history of Japanese theater or to announce the Harvard-Yale game, I would forget to show up for the first class or I would show up naked. That dream in particular seemed to me a woman's dream. Women are not bred to authority, I thought.

If I set myself up as an authority, people will see I'm a fraud.

At this time, the early 1970s, I found myself at a New Haven dinner party seated next to a Yale geologist who was about to retire after a long and distinguished teaching career. Professor Flint told me that there were many things he would miss about teaching, but one thing he would not miss: the nightmares he had at the start of every semester in which he presented himself at the podium for the first lecture and discovered he was naked.

Perhaps we should all have tapes of loved ones telling us the stories of our lives in mythic form—how the fleet massed and so on—just as Olympic athletes have think-positive tapes prescribed by their sports psychologists. Few of us need tapes to remind us how insignificant we are. The anxieties speak for themselves. There was a Roman emperor who had a slave at his side all the time to remind him he was mortal. But probably more of us are like George Eliot, who, according to her companion, needed a slave at her side constantly whispering, "You are not a noodle."

A G A I N S T   N O I S E

Spring brings many good things: baseball, daffodils, longer days, and lower heating bills. Yet I greet it with ambivalence. For when the silence of winter is gone, the sound of stereo is heard in the land.

I live across the street from a college dormitory. I love peace and quiet and believe I have a right to them. The students love loud music and believe they have a right to it. This is war. No sooner do I hear the opening thumps of distant music than I'm on the phone to the university police: "I want to register a complaint!"

Because I register so many complaints about noise from the dormitory, the students once delegated a resident adviser to speak with me. He was a sociology major, polite and articulate, named Eric.

Eric began by saying that we were all members of

a community and had to work to get along. The students knew they had a responsibility to their neighbors. They would not dream, for example, of playing loud music after one in the morning. I, for my part, should be sensitive to the role that music played in life. Today's college students were under great pressure and needed music to relax. Music helped create a community. It took people out of their book-centered isolation. He, for one, urged students to share their music with others.

Trying to match his earnestness, I told Eric that music made a spurious bond, and the real ties in an intellectual community like ours came from a shared commitment to the life of the mind. The life of the mind, I said, could not take place to rock music. Eric said it could. Some students, he said, could work only to music. Pulling rank, I said I knew more about the life of the mind than he did, and my mind couldn't function when it was assaulted by noise. "Music," said Eric.

"Don't get me wrong," I said. "I love music. It's listening to other people's music I object to. Let's say it's true that students work better to music. Why can't they listen through headphones? Why blast it out the window? Anyone who can afford stereo equipment can afford headphones." He reminded me of the function of music in creating a community. He went so far as to imply that it was unnatural to want to listen to music alone. He made me wonder if I really wanted a community or just a quiet place to live.

Quickly we moved into deep philosophical waters. Didn't a student have a right to enjoy himself in the privacy of his own room? Not when it conflicted with my right to enjoy peace and quiet in the privacy of my house. I found myself citing John Stuart Mill on the limits of liberty. As soon as I could hear it, their music became noise. He said I was overly sensitive and no fair test. At an impasse, we smiled, shook hands, and parted.

If you suffer from noise, as I do, you are always getting into fights. One winter my friend Danny and I spent several days at a small hotel on St. Lucia in the Caribbean. It was remote, hard to get to. And quiet? You might expect so. But on our first day, under the coconut-palm-thatched umbrella next to ours, a group of young people relaxed with a stereo cassette recorder playing full tilt. I asked them to turn down their music and they courteously did, although they seemed amazed at my request. My fight was with Danny. He didn't think I had the right to ask them to lower the volume. He thinks the beach is a public place: they have as much right to listen to music as I do to read a book. It's up to me to carve out of this public place the eccentric silence I desire.

I am lucky to be battling this issue with students and nice people on Caribbean beaches. Other people do not discuss objections to their listening habits with so much gentility and reason. Christopher Walken, the actor, strolling in New York City, was distressed by the loud music from two other pedestrians' portable cassette recorder. He asked them to turn down their music and they broke his finger.

Why hasn't the Walkman solved these problems? You can have your music and I can have my quiet. Eric, the sociology major, gave one answer: people like to hear music in groups. Another answer is that some people like to disturb others. To impose your music on others is to impose yourself. Loud music in a public place is a way of swaggering—macho, aggressive. It's hardly ever women students who play loud music out their windows.

Asking people to turn down their music is like asking them to turn down their personalities. I suspect that women may do better in this kind of confrontation than men. If a woman asks a man to turn down his music, it's a tribute to his strength. If a man asks him to turn it down, it's an insult. In court the music lovers who broke Mr. Walken's finger said in their own defense that Mr. Walken had not asked them to turn down their music politely enough.

I remind myself that, in regard to noise, things were no better in the past. Thomas Carlyle, the nineteenth-century British sage, was so disturbed by city noises that he built a soundproof room for himself at the top of his house in London. City noises then included the crowing of cocks, the rumbling of wheels over cobblestones, street cries from vendors, and the distant sound of train whistles—not rock music, but grating nonetheless. Walt Whitman in his later years was tormented by the choir of a Methodist church, a woman playing a piano, factory whistles, trains, and fife-and-drum brigades on the Fourth of July. It's an illusion to think that the past was silent, easier on the nerves.

Nor is nature much better. Ever been awakened by birds? Ever tried to think during a tropical rainstorm? Or to sleep when a neighbor's dog was barking? Ever tried to get rid of all the tree frogs around a Wellfleet pond so that you could have some peace? I know a man who shot a bluejay that was keeping him from reading *Miss Lonelyhearts*; he remembers the episode with mingled guilt and satisfaction: "I felt terrible about killing the bird. On the other hand, it's the only time I've won a battle for quiet."

Once you get worked up about it, every noise is a personal affront. This is dangerous when other people are involved. It's dangerous to raise the question "Who is more important?" Who is more important, Carlyle or the woman raising roosters next door? A student into Aerosmith or a teacher into *Arrowsmith?* You or me? We can be driven bananas by tree frogs but not hold their noise against them personally. We can even shoot an isolated bluejay and (Coleridge and his albatross notwithstanding) leave the moral order of the cosmos undisturbed. But when the prickliness of the noise lovers is matched by the prickliness of the noise minders, the war of all against all, I fear, is not far off.

The television show *People's Court* signs off with a line that gives me the chills. If you feel you've been wronged, don't take the law into your own hands; "take them to court." It gives me the chills because it suggests a society in which people have no way of settling disputes except by force or recourse to law. What about joking, jollying, bullying, grinning and bearing it? Why is there no standard of civilized behavior to which we can appeal?

OF SHOPPING

Last year a new Waldbaum's Food Mart opened in the shopping mall on Route 66. It belongs to a new generation of superdupermarkets that have computerized checkouts and operate twenty-four hours a day. I went to see the place as soon as it opened and I was impressed. There was trail mix in Lucite bins. There was freshly made pasta. There were coffee beans, four kinds of tahini, ten kinds of herb teas, raw shrimp in shells and cooked shelled shrimp, fresh-squeezed orange juice. Every sophistication known to the big city, even goat's cheese covered with ash, was now available in Middletown, Connecticut. People raced from the warehouse aisle to the bagel bin to the coffee beans to the fresh fish market, exclaiming at all the new things. Many of us felt elevated, graced, complimented by the presence of this food palace in our town.

This is the wonderful egalitarianism of American business. Was it Andy Warhol who said that the nice thing about Coke is, no can is any better or worse than any other? Some people may find it dull to cross the country and find the same chain stores with the same merchandise from coast to coast, but it means that my town is as good as yours, my shopping mall as important as yours, equally filled with wonders.

Imagine what people ate during the winter as little as seventy-five years ago. They ate food that was local, long-lasting, and dull, like acorn squash, turnips, and cabbage. Walk into an American supermarket in February and the world lies before you: grapes, melons, artichokes, fennel, lettuce, peppers, pistachios, dates, even strawberries, to say nothing of ice cream. Have you ever considered what a triumph of civilization it is to be able to buy a pound of chicken livers? If you lived on a farm and had to kill a chicken when you wanted to eat one, you wouldn't ever accumulate a pound of chicken livers.

Another wonder of Middletown is Caldor, the discount department store. Here is man's plenty: tennis racquets, pantyhose, luggage, glassware, records, toothpaste, Timex watches, Cadbury's chocolate, corn poppers, hair dryers, warm-up suits, car wax, light bulbs, television sets. All good quality at low prices with exchanges cheerfully made on defective goods. There are worse rules to live by. I feel good about America whenever I walk into this store, which is almost every midwinter Sunday afternoon, when life elsewhere has closed down. I go to Caldor the way English people go to pubs: out of sociability. To get away from my house. To widen my horizons. For culture's sake. Caldor provides me too with a welcome sense of seasonal change. When the first outdoor grills and lawn furniture appear there, it's as exciting a sign of spring as the first crocus or robin.

Someone told me about a Soviet émigré who practices English by declaiming, at random, sentences that catch his fancy. One of his favorites is "Fifty percent off all items today only." Refugees from Communist countries appreciate our supermarkets and discount department stores for the wonders they are. An Eastern European scientist visiting Middletown wept when she first saw the meat counter at Waldbaum's. On the other hand, before her year in America was up, her pleasure turned sour. She wanted everything she saw. Her approach to consumer goods was insufficiently abstract, too materialistic. We Americans are beyond a simple, possessive materialism. We're used to abundance and the possibility of possessing things. The things, and the possibility of possessing them, will still be there next week, next year. So today we can walk the aisles calmly.

It is a misunderstanding of the American retail store to think we go there necessarily to buy. Some of us shop. There's a difference. Shopping has many purposes, the least interesting of which is to acquire new articles. We shop to cheer ourselves up. We shop to practice decision making. We shop to be useful and productive members of our class and society. We shop to remind ourselves how much is available to us. We shop to remind ourselves how much is to be striven for. We shop to assert our superiority to the material objects that spread themselves before us.

Shopping's function as a form of therapy is widely appreciated. You don't really need, let's say, another sweater. You need the feeling of power that comes with buying it or not buying it. You need the feeling that someone wants something you have—even if it's just your money. To get the benefit of shopping, you needn't actually purchase the sweater, any more than you have to marry every man you flirt with. In fact, window shopping, like flirting, can be more rewarding, the same high without the distressing commitment, the material encumbrance. The purest form of shopping is provided by garage sales. A connoisseur goes out with no goal in mind, open to whatever may come his way, secure that it will cost very little. Minimum expense, maximum experience. Perfect shopping.

I try to think of the opposite, a kind of shopping in which the object is all-important, the pleasure of shopping at a minimum. For example, the purchase of blue jeans. I buy new blue jeans as seldom as possible because the experience is so humiliating. For every pair that looks good on me, fifteen look grotesque. But even shopping for blue jeans at Bob's Surplus on Main Street—no-frills, bare-bones shopping—is an event in the life of the spirit. Once again I have to come to terms with the fact that I will never look good in Levi's. Much as I want to be mainstream, I will never be.

In fact, I'm doubly an oddball, neither Misses nor Junior, but Misses Petite. I look in the mirror, I acknowledge the disparity between myself and the ideal, I resign myself to making the best of it: I will buy the Lee's Misses Petite. Shopping is a time of reflection, assessment, spiritual self-discipline.

It is appropriate, I think, that Bob's has a communal dressing room. I used to shop only in places where I could count on a private dressing room with a mirror inside. My impulse was to hide my weaknesses. Now I believe in sharing them. There are other women in the dressing room at Bob's trying on blue jeans who look as bad as I do. We take comfort in one another. Sometimes a woman will ask me which of two items looks better. I always give a definite answer. It's the least I can do. I figure we are all in this together, and I emerge from the dressing room not only with a new pair of jeans, but with a renewed sense of belonging to a human community.

When a Solzhenitsyn rants about American materialism, I have to look at my digital Timex and check what year this is. Materialism? Like conformism, a hot moral issue of the 1950s, but not now. How to spread the goods, maybe. Whether the goods are the Good, no. Solzhenitsyn, like the visiting scientist who wept at the beauty of the Waldbaum's meat counter but came to covet everything she saw, takes American materialism too materialistically. He doesn't see its spiritual side. Caldor, Waldbaum's, Bob's—these, perhaps, are our cathedrals.

THE TRAGIC FLAW

I once taught the freshman Great Books course at Wesleyan University. Its official title is Touchstones of Western Values, and my students were eager to get as many values as possible. One complained that although the course covered the *Iliad*, Greek tragedy, Socratic dialogues, and the Bible, it included no Roman values. I answered his consumerist complaint with a consumerist explanation: next year, when Robert Fitzgerald's translation appeared in paperback, we would "cover" the *Aeneid*.

Ten years before, in the 1970s, when I had last taught the course, it was struggling to survive widespread skepticism about canonical lists of great books and the value of Western civilization. We taught Malraux's *Man's Fate* along with the *Iliad* and Sartre's *The Flies* along with the *Oresteia* in order to give the ancient works what we did not blush to call "contemporary relevance." On the whole I preferred the consumerism. I was relieved not to have to defend daily the ground I walked on, as we had had to do in the days when undergraduates laughed at the idea of a course on Great Books or Western Values.

My usual stamping ground was English literature, so my knowledge of the classical material was not profound. But the ability to read a text responsibly kept me ahead of my students, who tended to treat all literature as a Rorschach test, on which they brought to bear the few ideas that were already firmly in their minds. Fair enough. That's why courses like this one exist. That's why education exists: to free people from their preconceptions, to introduce them to something outside the self, to keep the objective world from being a giant Rorschach test.

The *Iliad* mystified my students. Most of them so distrusted military actions that they could hardly see this one as an occasion for glory. Nor could they wrap their minds around the idea that a short life with glory might be more desirable than a long life without glory. Given that choice—a short life with glory or a long life without it—Achilles chose glory. I took a vote on the same question. All but three of my twenty-three students chose long life. They seemed to feel that if the ancient Greeks had lived with nuclear disaster around the corner, they would have had more respect for long life. Glory was decidedly a luxury item.

The *Iliad* was alien to them also because of the gods, who take sides, intrude, play tricks, and generally behave in an undignified fashion. My students had the exaggerated respect for other people's gods characteristic of those who have no gods themselves. They assumed that gods should behave seriously to be taken seriously, should behave admirably in order to inspire us to do the same. The Greek gods and goddesses disappointed them by joking around. Gradually they came to feel that the whole Trojan War was the fault of the gods. I argued in vain that the gods should be seen as literary expressions of passions and powers existing inside man. My students remained fatalistic. The gods—a bad lot—were to blame.

I shocked them by revealing my preference for Trojans over Greeks. The Trojans, I explained, are represented as people of culture and refined sensibilities. The Greeks are comparative barbarians. To my horrified students, this opinion flew in the face of history. After all, the Greeks won. They must be better.

This brings us to the heart of the matter, the irreducible difference between my students and the ancient Greeks. Deep down, my students, cockeyed optimists all, believed that good prevails and only the bad die young. They believed in justice. If you had asked them directly, they might have denied it, but their belief in justice came out in discussion.

It came out particularly when we discussed the tragic flaw. Good high schools across America apparently teach young people that a tragedy is tragic because a good man is led to destruction inevitably through some flaw in his character. If he didn't have a flaw, it wouldn't be tragic because it wouldn't "mean" anything. It would just be bad luck. To convince students that bad luck isn't tragic must take some fancy teaching; people without education tend to believe that bad luck is precisely what tragedy is about. But by the time they reach me, they're convinced.

Subscribing to the tragic-flaw theory has in fact become a hallmark of the educated person, the humanistic equivalent of belief in a just God. So my students, who had traded up from their one-dollar idea that tragedy concerns unhappy events to the ten-dollar notion that tragedy results from a flaw in the hero's character, offered me their belief in the tragic flaw and expected to be praised. I was outraged. I think the idea of the tragic flaw is one of the worst ever to come down the pike. It encourages self-satisfaction and the turning of one's back on other people's problems.

My students said "if only" a lot. If only Macbeth hadn't been so ambitious, if only this or that had been avoided, everything would have been fine. "Everything is never fine," I told them. None of us gets out of this alive. Tragedy is built into life. I adopted the metaphor of my material: "Zeus keeps two jars by his doorway— one filled with good, one with evil. He throws down both indiscriminately." There's no "if only" about it.

Oedipus was my ace in the hole, because I thought there's no way he can be seen as deserving his fate. An oracle has prophesied that he will sleep with his mother and kill his father, so, horrified at the prospect of committing these crimes, he leaves the people he thinks are his parents. Of course, he runs smack into his real parents and commits the crimes he had been fleeing from. But how can he be seen as morally responsible? My students said he should never have left Corinth. He shouldn't have tried to escape the prophecy. His tragic flaw was arrogance. He flew off the handle. He shouldn't have killed that guy at the crossroads. Under the circumstances, he shouldn't have gone to bed with any woman without investigating very carefully whether or not she was his mother.

Our willingness to believe that people who have had bad luck somehow deserve it is a depressing fact of human nature. The tragic-flaw idea spills over from art to life. Throughout the semester I mentioned appalling news items. Three people were burned to death in a summer house on Fire Island. Was someone smoking in bed? asks a student. Did they have the electrical system checked recently? In a heavy rain, Jessica Savitch and her companion drowned when their car overturned in a canal. Had they been drinking? If illness, evil, and death are not punishments, life is too frightening to consider. If there's no way of winning the game, who wants to play?

I ended the semester convinced of the "relevance" of the classical texts if their vision of the essential injustice of human life can be made to prevail. I fielded them against the moralistic consolations that protect my students' minds. But it was hard going, and sometimes, in my bad moments, I feared I was merely substituting a hundred-dollar disbelief for the ten-dollar ideas my students had come to me with.

OF EDUCATION

Walter Jackson Bate, whose massive and magnificent biography of Samuel Johnson was published in 1977, was one of my teachers when I was an undergraduate. Whenever I think about education, I end up thinking about him.

Bate was in his mid-forties when I was at Radcliffe. Already he was considered a Great Man, one of the Harvard English Department's luminaries, along with Douglas Bush, Harry Levin, and Reuben Brower. He had already published a good deal, including *The Achievement of Samuel Johnson*, a moving book that seemed definitive at the time but was—one can say in retrospect—merely a warm-up for the later volume. In 1963, at about the time I was taking The Age of

Johnson, his large undergraduate lecture course, Bate published his critical biography of Keats, a model of the genre.

The Age of Johnson was an undergraduate favorite, always well enrolled and well attended. I remember several times leaving the lecture hall and walking with fellow students across the street to continue over a cup of coffee discussions initiated by Bate's lectures. Naturally, since we admired him, we all made fun of Professor Bate. We considered him a parody professor: he smoked a pipe; he wore baggy clothes; he shuffled and looked at his feet when he walked; he affected Samuel Johnson's melancholy and was constantly sighing. Since he wasn't married, we speculated on whether or not he was gay. Some of us who had read *The Achievement of Samuel Johnson* were aware that parts of his lectures were lifted bodily from the book. This irritated us. It seemed like cheating. And yet, so splendid a lecturer was he that even if you had already read the words, they still gave you a chill when you heard him speak them. It was a joke among us that Bate had been making students cry over the death of Johnson, half crying himself as he lectured, for ten years, same time every year.

We knew that, despite the number of times he had had to articulate his thoughts to succeeding generations of students, Bate took Johnson seriously. Phrases like "the hunger of the imagination" and "the stability of truth" meant something to him, which he explored in his writing and which connected with his life. The historian Kevin Starr, a former Bate student, has speculated that one reason for the perennial popularity of Bate's course was that it satisfied "an old-fashioned, unappeased hunger for religious ideas and moral philosophy" in an undoctrinaire and nonproselytizing fashion. I think this is true.

Bate conveyed his belief that literature, read thoughtfully, could help you live better. You emerged from his course with an appreciation of the dignity of reason, or, more precisely, of the attempt to be reasonable. You emerged with an appreciation of the virtues of clarity and order and also the value of keeping yourself merely busy, in the hope that something useful might take shape from activity, whereas, out of sloth, nothing but further despair could grow. You were left, finally, with a tragic view of humanity in which the struggle to impose order and meaning on existence *was* a struggle, and success, if achieved at all, was precarious and transient. There was nothing abstract or formulaic about this. Bate seemed to be living it before your eyes.

So, while we put his lectures down as histrionic, too entertaining, we never missed a class. We went away talking about the hunger of the imagination and how, with the pleasures of sudden wonder soon exhausted, the mind could rest only upon the stability of truth. Even if one were to put the lowest possible value on it and dismiss what Bate did for us as mere entertainment, one would have to distinguish between the quality of entertainment offered by a Bate and that purveyed by—let us say—mud wrestlers. To be entertained by Bate talking about Samuel Johnson, to pursue the discussion of truth, reason, and imagination from the classroom to the coffee house, is precisely "the life of the mind" that colleges exist to nurture and facilitate.

On the surface, I did not do well in Bate's course. My grade was C+. In fact, I had been unable to bring myself to write more than half of the final exam and had left the exam room after the first hour. My parents were puzzled by that anomalous grade on my record, but I've never been ashamed of it. If anything, quite the opposite. To me, in some strange reversal, it proved the success of the course.

The "facts" of literature in the age of Johnson have disappeared from my mind. I cannot name ten minor poets of the time. I cannot recall Johnson's ideas about envy. I cannot even tell you exactly when the age of Johnson was. The facts are finally trivial—and evanescent. One is left with something weightier, at once more and less palpable than facts: a feeling for order, or for the dangerous generativity of chaos; an increased sensitivity to certain of the beauties—material and spiritual—in life, or of its disgraces. Or, perhaps, one is left with a model, an embodiment of ideals in the form of a somewhat laughable professor obsessed with a theory, an era, a person, a book. Beneath the ostensible subject of any good course there is always that buried possibility and hope, that the more important thing will be found, that the student's individual and idiosyncratic need for aesthetic, moral, intellectual meaning will be mobilized. Dance can do it, calligraphy, biology, mathematics: the "hardest" subjects sometimes turn out to have nothing at the core and the "softest" to be the most solid.

When I was a senior, I enrolled in a studio course in photography. My father refused to pay my tuition unless I dropped the course. He said that he was not spending so much money for me to take frivolous courses like that. I complied, dropped the course, and substituted—with tongue-in-cheek private defiance— the driest course I could find, The History of the English Language. As it turned out, I got a lot from the course, proving my point: you never know where spirit will be hidden. But I hoped that some time I would be able to explain to my father, a gambler who always bet against the table, the peculiar gambles of my education.

MARKING TIME:
GRADUATIONS

On my way out the door to Jenny's graduation, I asked my teenage son if he had any messages for his cousin. "Tell her I envy her," he said. "Tell her I wish I was graduating from college." I should have replied with my own mother's homily: "Don't wish your life away." At graduation, the place was crawling with kids who wished they were older and grownups who wished they were younger. In fact, one view of graduation is that it marks the shifting of a group of people from the former category to the latter, from yearners to nostalgics. When I told my niece that Teddy envied her graduating from college, she said she envied him, having it ahead of him. In middle-class America, the biggest fence on the other side of which the grass is greener is college graduation.

So the jokes of the graduation speaker seemed more fraught to me than I suspect he intended them to be. He quoted Bob Hope: "As you stand here on the brink of your future, about to leave these hallowed halls for the rough world outside, I have one thing to say to you. DON'T GO!" Art Buchwald: "My generation has given you a perfect world. Don't screw it up!" Woody Allen: "You stand at a crossroads in your lives. It is up to you to choose between the path of despair and misery and the path of utter annihilation."

The speaker, Senator Christopher Dodd of Connecticut, showed his good sense of history by mentioning the year these graduating seniors were born— 1964, the year, he reminded us, of the Civil Rights Act, the year the Warren Commission declared Oswald the sole killer of Kennedy, the year of the Gulf of Tonkin Resolution and the beginning of Johnson's war on poverty. Also, although Senator Dodd did not say so, the year of my graduation from college. If the speaker at my graduation had had the same wit as Senator Dodd, he would have mentioned the great events of the year of my birth, like the invasion of North Africa, so that my parents could savor, as I did at Jenny's graduation, the passing of time and the way it is intersected by the great recurring events of individual life.

As a professor, I get to go to more than my share of graduations, but they never fail to move me. I like them because they change something fundamental about the campus. Usually, there is an unnatural stasis about a college campus. Time stops here. The students are always between eighteen and twenty-one. I age, but they don't. Nor, cumulatively, do they learn. As soon as they've mastered whatever I have to teach, I pass them on and get a new batch of innocents. At graduation, the narrow band of age represented on a college campus resumes its place in the spectrum. The single note of youth takes its place in the chord. There are the students, the parents, the grandparents, the babies, gathered in wooden folding chairs on the lawn. It's a flower arrangement as it should be, with flowers in different stages, some buds, some in full bloom, and some shriveling, about to drop.

Every graduation provokes in me a meditation on time. Time seems the presiding deity. Jenny's graduation took place under an enormous bronze statue of Thomas Church Brownell, the first president of Trinity College. As the proceedings oozed along and the three hundredth senior was presented with a diploma, I went into a trance in which the statue of Brownell became a figure of Time; "Time, the subtle thief of youth," an allegorical figure, pointing his finger at the graduating seniors like Uncle Sam in the draft posters, saying, "I want you—and I will have you"; Time, which heaps experience, wanted or not, is the ultimate teacher.

When I feel cynical, the gradual detachment of students from their families seems to me the chief purpose of college. I notice that freshmen return to school after their first visit home at Thanksgiving significantly more "grown up," that is, distanced from their families and closer to their friends than before. For parents, too, there is a process of detachment. Just as the cost of psychotherapy is supposed to be part of the cure (a token of how much your own health is worth to you), the very expense of college may be part of the process of detachment. By the time they finish paying for college, parents need feel no guilt about letting go. This stately progression toward maturity, in which college plays such a crucial part, is peculiarly American. Whether it makes us more mature is another question.

A freshman at Wesleyan said with a passion I'll never forget, "I want my life to begin." Useless to tell him it already had. I thought I knew what he meant. He was protesting against sitting in classes and reading books when he wanted to be out in the world making money, making love, making a name for himself. And surely he was old enough to. Dickens never went to college. At fourteen he was supporting himself as a reporter. To say nothing of Andrew Carnegie. What answer could I give to "I want my life to begin"? What was a competent eighteen-year-old doing in a holding tank?

But when I am not feeling cynical, I think that education lets us put up a better fight against Time. By training young people to read, education releases them from the need to learn everything from experience. By training them to think, it frees them from having to follow the conventions of the past. When I'm not feeling cynical, I think it is a beautiful thing to create so elaborate a system to give our children intellectual as well as emotional independence.

I approve of the current tendency to use graduation as a platform for political statement. The real business of graduation, the honoring of Time, goes on underneath, no matter what words are spoken, what advice given, what banners waved. It is built into the structure of the event, the way the families gather to pay tribute to their young. It is made concrete in the way the graduates sit, dressed differently, a somber block, all the same age, separate from the colorful multiplicity of the rest of the audience. It's appropriate they should voice a collective protest before each starts squawking, each in his or her own way, against the inexorable injustices of Time.

MARKING TIME:
REUNIONS

I thought I didn't have many friends in my college class, but at my twentieth reunion many people looked familiar. I had forgotten the number of hours I spent chatting in dorm rooms with women who mean nothing to me now. I was interested in everything then. Everyone was potentially fascinating. At the same time, I quickly discarded people who failed to hold my interest. In one way or another many of us were snobs, impatient with any group that was not the one we were looking for. Now, all a person has to do is look familiar to be a welcome sight, and the entire class is our group. No more snobs.

Looking at old friends, unseen for twenty years, I have frequently on my face the idiot grin of surprise, wonder, and pleasure you see when people look at a baby: the process works. Put a man and woman together and you get a baby who looks a little like each of them. Susie R, Susie B, Penny, Lisa, and Sarah look exactly as they did twenty years ago, yet they look forty, not twenty. The process works. Add twenty years to a face, and it's the same face, only twenty years older. Olivia brought her son, eight years old— additional proof that the process works. He looks just like Olivia. "Molly, Millie—same thing watered down" was Leopold Bloom's succinct description of this phenomenon as it affected his wife and daughter.

Nobody changes. The charmer of twenty years ago is still a charmer. The sourpuss, still a sourpuss. The woman who drove me crazy twenty years ago by smiling all the time still smiles, still wears the same baby blue cotton shirt with the circle pin. Georgia is still adorable but flaky; Carol still reckless. The metaphor for personality is a flowering. Our personalities don't develop. They are simply, at this stage of our lives, full-blown. In another twenty years, we'll be the same but tattered.

We all want to talk about our parents. Twenty years ago, we didn't. We were too intent on being ourselves and separating from them to want to consider their influence on us. They were just the toehold from which the race had started. The race was the thing. Now we are enthralled by the chain of life. Betsy launches into a bitter tale of resentment. Her mother did everything too well—worked all day, yet insisted on making dinner, to exercise control. Betsy at forty-one is taking an odd revenge by getting the best medical care she can for her now ailing mother. Margaret reveals that she was never allowed to have a radio, a TV, or what she calls a "victrola." Her parents married late, were isolated. She was never allowed to date. Her sister cried when someone kissed her for the first time in her last year of college. "I had a lot to overcome," says Margaret. In college I remember thinking her a prude.

At a reunion, everyone has a story. This is what we've all worked to collect, a life different from other lives, a personal history, a narrative. "I am an opera singer. I had a good career in Europe but I met the man of my dreams and decided to marry him. The last train was pulling out. Now I have a four-year-old daughter. In three years, we are going to sail around the world." And: "I am a first-year medical student. I married right out of college and raised three kids. I've had a good life with my family. But now I'd like to do more. My daughter is a figure skater. I drive her to the rink every day. It's hard to do all these things, but rewarding."

Your story is your individuality, but curiously, when you've heard just a few of these stories, they don't sound all that different. A life is a life. One's individuality is a satisfaction only to oneself. Which is why all the autobiographical accounts in reunion books have a hard time avoiding self-congratulation. Who besides X can care much that she was nominated for the National Book Award or is vice-president in charge of marketing for General Foods?

The democracy of the healthy family—no child is more important than any other, no matter what he or she has accomplished—applies also to a reunion class, despite the crude efforts of an inevitable few to impress the rest with their achievements. If you really feel you have wasted your life and have nothing to show for yourself, you don't go to a reunion. If you go, then your three children count as much as the next person's career in the foreign service.

We go to reunions to tell our stories, to display our painfully acquired individuality, but their strongest message is that we belong to a group. We have been soldiers in the same war and bond with the fellowship of the trenches. We are rafting down the river of time together; we hit the rapids at the same moment. We all think of Kennedy's assassination as the extended present, not the past. The past is World War II. The same great things happen to us at more or less the same time. We like each other now because we shared that four-year moment of intensity twenty years ago. Whatever our individual accomplishments, our most significant accomplishment is having made it through twenty years. The only stories of real interest are those of the ones who didn't, the ones who died: Jo, who died in a fire; Jonathan, who was electrocuted; Bruce, who was killed by a junkie; Frances, whom cancer took.

I had made a tape of 1950s songs—"Earth Angel," "Rock Around the Clock," "That'll Be the Day"—and played it for my friends. This was the music we danced to in seventh grade and early high school. Those had not been pleasant years for most of us. We had sat out too many dances. But now, listening to the tape, we thought fondly of seventh-grade parties. Memory works on the past beneficially, filtering out the boredom, the irritation, the grit, and saving mostly golden moments. In college I used to feel bitter when my parents told me those were the best years of my life. For me, they were a vale of tears, charged with perilous friendship, frustrated ambition, overwork, and failed romance. Now I look back and perceive their glamour and privilege. If life can be savored only in retrospect, it's a good thing we have reunions.

EYESORES AND
IVORY TOWERS

During reunion weekend at Yale in 1988, an alumnus, class of '58, burned the shanties on Beinecke Plaza that undergraduates had erected some two years before as a protest against apartheid. Another alumnus, class of '68, saw him flee the scene, pursued, and caught him. "You're in a lot of trouble," the pursuer told the arsonist. "I hope you've got a good lawyer. This is a democracy and you don't do that sort of thing."

I used to pass the shanties on my way to the Beinecke Library. Constructed of cardboard and spare pieces of lumber, they were supposed to represent the shacks imposed upon the poor black workers of South Africa by the racist white power structure. They were very ugly. I thought I understood how angry it made Dr. Elwood Bracey of West Palm Beach, the arsonist, to see his beloved alma mater defaced by the eyesore. What right did those students have to clutter up the Yale landscape with their self-righteous political statement?

In saying "This is a democracy. You don't do that sort of thing," Dr. Michael Charney, the captor, implied that the people who erected the shanties were expressing an opinion, and anyone who cancels the statement they made is violating their freedom of expression. But what about the arsonist's freedom of expression? Wasn't he expressing his opinion by burning down the eyesore? Naturally there's a difference between a spoken opinion and an opinion translated into destructive action, but hadn't that distinction already been blurred by the building of the shanties? Does freedom of expression include the right to build anything you want anywhere you want it?

No one consults us about the buildings we have to live in sight of. A twelve-story skyscraper has just pierced the skyline of my heretofore low-lying hometown. To me it is a terrible eyesore, which changes the way the town looks from miles around. Did anyone ask us townsfolk if we wanted it? The new Citicorp building in Queens is visible the length of Manhattan's East Side, and certainly from my mother's window. Did anyone ask her if she wanted her view destroyed by this skyscraper?

When you get right down to it, Beinecke Plaza itself is no thing of beauty, a treeless stone extravaganza edged in monumental styles. To compensate for its lack of vitality, a tradition has grown of using the space for art. The shanties shared the plaza with an Alexander Calder. But back in the seventies this was the site of Claes Oldenburg's enormous vinyl sculpture of a lipstick whose "case" was a tank, a witty commentary on war and the relationship between weapons and the masculine mystique. When the Vietnam War was over, the sculpture seemed to have outlived its usefulness and was moved. No less than Oldenburg's lipstick, the shanties were political sculpture. I don't know whether the students who built them would have called them "art," but they were certainly a "statement," intended to affect the way people felt.

Beinecke Plaza's buildings—the library, the vast, columned dining hall, the Beaux Arts concert hall—make their own political statements. The dining hall, which bears carved in stone the names of the great World War I battles in which Yale alumni died, celebrates the connection between the university and history. In contrast, the Skidmore, Owings and Merrill library, in which marble panels replace windows and give the impression of a building that has turned its back completely on the outside world, celebrates the university's insularity. The sunken sculpture garden by Noguchi asserts through its marble sphere, cube, and pyramid that the verities of form are eternal and that the life of the mind pursues its goals beyond historical circumstance. One way or another the grandiose buildings around Beinecke Plaza express the power, wealth, and authority of a great university.

Throughout the years, many members of the university have believed that it exists apart from history, beyond ideology. Beinecke Plaza, a formalist chef d'oeuvre, expresses that delusion of neutrality as the shanties protested it. If the university is the Olympian endeavor these buildings want to say it is, it is so only precariously. Left to themselves, the stones speak a message not so much of neutrality as of supercilious nonengagement, of being comfortably on the side of power and wealth.

Bracey and Charney, arsonist and pursuer, '58 individualist and '68 moralist, illustrate how mythical is the university's continuity, its existence outside history. Dr. Charney and Dr. Bracey may both sing "The Whiffenpoof Song," but they went to different colleges. They had different classmates, different educations, different faculties. What was white, male, Anglo-Saxon Protestant or Irish in 1958 had by 1968 started to become the part-black, part-female, part-Jewish body it is now, which increasingly views art as an honorific bestowed by Western culture on those objects which embody its values.

If Oldenburg's lipstick says something we want said, it is art. If not, it's an eyesore. A weed is a flower you don't want growing in your garden. Dr. Bracey saw something he didn't want in his garden and pulled it up. Only it wasn't his garden anymore.

ON MAKING SENSE

In October I got a Christmas card. On the front, a picture of a puppy in a fur-trimmed cap and the words "Especially for you, Mother." Inside, a poem: "This Christmas wish is special / With a warm and loving touch / Because it's for a mother / Who is loved so very much. MERRY CHRISTMAS." Although the card was unsigned and bore no return address, I knew who sent it: a former student of mine—the same person who, a month before, had smashed a window of my house and pitched garbage through the hole. This much too early Christmas card carried a message, but I knew it wasn't "Merry Christmas."

The scary thing about madness is that it makes perfect sense to the person who's mad. My former student thought he was telling me that I was concerned too exclusively with English literature. That's why, he said, he broke my kitchen window: it faces east. He didn't consider it an act of violence. Everyone knows that the sun never sets on the British Empire, but how many people care where it rises? It rises in the east. Therefore, he explained, he bashed in my eastern window. There's no doubt his act was symbolic, because he could have walked in through the kitchen's open door to deposit his garbage. The only problem: my kitchen window faces west.

When the attack came, I was upstairs with a friend picking out a color to paint the hall. We heard glass crashing; I thought, "A picture has fallen off the wall." The crashing continued. "Two pictures have fallen," I thought. As the crashing went on, it got harder to make sense of it. We ran down to the kitchen in time to see glass fragments flying off the edge of a jagged hole in the window, then an arm reaching through, throwing in glass, beer bottles, junk.

I confronted him. He looked like Z, a young man I'd particularly liked, who had baby-sat for my son, whom I'd once had to dinner with his girlfriend. But Z smiled and had expressive eyes; this person's mouth was tightly set, his eyes fixed. I didn't believe it was Z until the university police arrived in response to my call and asked to see his driver's license. It was Z but not Z: a humorless obsessive had somehow taken over his body.

I asked, "Why did you do this? I thought we were friends." He said, "Because of your writing. Also, I was disappointed with your course." No smile followed this remark.

Each piece of garbage meant something, he told me. He had spent six hours searching the garbage cans of Middletown for certain beer bottles, Popsicle sticks, and just the right wrappers. Each item was a specific reply to an idea I'd expressed, and together they constituted a "text." He thought when I'd "read" the message on my kitchen floor, I would want to discuss it with him further. For five years, since he'd taken my course on the history of the English novel, he'd been carrying on a conversation with me in his mind on the relationship between life and art. He had taken the train from New York to continue that conversation by breaking my window, although I hadn't talked to him in years.

"Why didn't you phone if you wanted to talk?" I asked. "If you don't like my work, write letters to the editor." But he had an answer for everything. It all made sense—to him. Too much made sense. He took things that had no meaning as signs and messages. It was important that the first thing he'd seen that morning was a picture of the Indian goddess Devi. The state of the Middle East, Heidegger, and my course five years before were all somehow connected.

Z insisted there was nothing wrong with his mind. Typical of me, he said bitterly, to suggest there was. When he was my student, I'd always urged him to make his writing less abstract. According to him, I called all serious thinking "out of touch with reality." To suggest he was disturbed was another of my refusals to engage in serious intellectual discussion, because what I called "out of touch with reality" he called "philosophy."

"I am holding you accountable for your writing," he said, words more chilling than usual when you don't know whether you're being held accountable for what you wrote or what he thinks you wrote. If garbage through my window means "Your view of literature is too Eurocentric," what does a Christmas card, "Especially for you, Mother," mean? Is there an ironic allusion to the fact that neither Z nor I celebrate Christmas? Could it point to a shared exclusion and thus represent a kind of apology? Does the puppy in the fur-trimmed hat implicate my dog? Who knows? I'm sure it all makes sense to him. At the time of John Hinckley's attack on President Reagan, a joke made the rounds: Why did Israel attack Lebanon? To impress Jodie Foster.

Virginia Woolf in *Mrs. Dalloway* portrays Septimus Warren Smith in his madness as wispy and fragmented. He imagines that Evans (dead since World War I) is alive and coming through the undergrowth; King Edward is muttering obscenities in the rose bushes; the birds are speaking Greek. But more alarming to me would be the conviction that everything is tied together, that the king's obscenities are replies to the birds' Greek, and if you said the right word to Evans—only the word would be an action, like throwing a magical Popsicle stick—all the chatter would stop and so would the war between Iran and Iraq.

"What if Z decides that coming at me with a hammer is not a hostile act but a message?" I asked a therapist I know.

The therapist said, "The poor kid. He needs help. He isn't dangerous to anyone but himself."

"Poor thing," I said, taking her cue. But I wasn't completely convinced I should be more worried about him than about me. My impulse was to get him locked up. If I called the town police, however, the charge would be vandalism, and he'd be free in a matter of hours. Also, the therapist said the experience might turn him from a harmless troubled person into a dangerous, paranoid one. Since he was no longer a student, the university police could do nothing except warn him away. This left me to try to forget it and get on with my life. But I couldn't forget.

For two or three weeks, it was hard not to wonder if I'd be attacked again that day. It was hard not to think about how little protection anyone has against being made a part of someone else's very private sense of what's wrong with the world. When you're under attack by someone who doesn't believe he's attacking you, you begin to raise questions about the nature of reality. How do you prove, except in effect by majority vote, what's real and what's crazy? Do more people agree with Z or with me? It comes down to that.

Until the blessed healthiness of oblivion took over, I talked to everyone who would listen about the crashing glass, the glazed eyes, the magical Popsicle sticks, the senseless explanations. Then I forgot what a miracle sanity is and regained the paradise of taking daily life for granted. Until the Christmas card arrived in October, starting the cycle of awareness and forgetting all over again.

PLAYING FOR KEEPS

When I heard that some women were having a jacks tournament last summer on Martha's Vineyard, I didn't hesitate: I invited myself and Wendy. Jacks! The very word was like a bell that tolled me back to childhood summers, to hour after hour (when time was not money) spent on the small concrete porches of our cabins at camp doing Cherry in the Basket, Flying Dutchman, and Over the Fence.

I hadn't so much as thought about jacks in thirty years. I couldn't believe that girls in 1988 were still playing the games we played in 1952. But when I went to the local general store, I found jacks aplenty, and pickup sticks too. I took them back to my rented house in Chilmark—a long way from the humble bunks of summer camp—eager to see if my hands remembered the moves.

My hands remembered, but moved slowly. I could see where to subtract the four from the pack to leave six, I could see the best dividing place between the one and the nine, but I couldn't swoop the jacks up before the ball plopped satisfyingly back into my hand after its bounce. The old hand-eye coordination wasn't what it had been. I kept messing up.

So it is. Age is a matter of realizing that the games of one's youth were demanding.

To an unsympathetic eye, we must have made a ridiculous spectacle, sitting on the nicely polished wood floor of a spacious living room in Vineyard Haven: two dozen middle-aged women playing like kids. We included a real estate broker, a literary agent, a dating-service tycoon, a couple of college professors, and several writers. Most of these women gathered several days a week to do Jane Fonda. They were in shape.

In exercise gear and the shorts of summer, we sat on the floor in the four classic positions: the V; the modified V, in which you bend one leg back at the knee and sit on it; the other modified V, in which you bend the second leg in front of you and lean over it; and the kneeling (crap-shooting) position. In the first morning's elimination round, each group of six women rendered up one champion. Then the four winners reduced themselves to two. When things got literally sticky, our hostess kindly powdered her floor with Givenchy talcum powder.

Wendy was one of the finalists. She swept through her basic moves and went quickly on to the variations. I had never seen her so concentrated on anything. Her rapport with the small red ball and the metal jacks was riveting, the relation of a musician to her instrument, a painter to her canvas. One onlooker said in wonder,

"Whatever you do, you have to be serious about it.'

If the Battle of Waterloo was won on the playing fields of Eton, credit should go to the floors and porches of America, on which the competitive instincts of generations of American women were honed by jacks. It seemed to me no accident that the two best players had both been educated at the Convent of the Sacred Heart. Those nuns taught their pupils to take being a woman seriously—and competitively. A Sacred Heart girl was supposed to prepare herself to marry the richest or most powerful man in sight. She played to win. Think of the fighting spirit she passed on to her sons!

Several women, who would never have boasted about any other accomplishment, told me how good they were at jacks. There was no feminine modesty or self-deprecation about it. I'd say that's because the game predated the age at which women learned to put themselves down in favor of men. Before the boy-girl time of adolescence, when deference was acquired and women's competitiveness was largely transferred to the service of their mates, a female world existed, and jacks was its sport of choice.

I offered to coach Wendy and to act as her manager in the playoff later that week. For two days, we practiced hard, on her polished wood floors and on mine.

Her friend Marina, raised in Europe, thought we were crazy. "What a waste of time!" she said. "I've always defended Americans against Europeans who said they were childish. But now I see you *are* childish. You will turn into the kind of women who spend their lives playing bridge."

Marina was off base. Boswell once tried to bait Dr. Johnson, the greatest moralist of all, into railing against people who played cards. Dr. Johnson wouldn't bite. "Life must be got through somehow," he said.

Moreover, there was something involved in this tournament that Marina, not brought up American, couldn't catch. Of course it was, like any sporting event, a celebration of hard work and concentration. But even more important, it was a rite of female solidarity.

Given the way social divisions prevail, especially in summer resorts, it was nice of these women from Vineyard Haven to welcome me and Wendy from Chilmark. But we had appealed to a higher bonding, a deeper association, a national female culture. Although we jacks players had grown up all over America, although we came from different classes and belonged to different religious and ethnic groups, we were united by jacks. This was a rite that had bound us as girls; this rite, recalled with irony, nostalgia, affection, continued to bind us as women.

People are always asking me to join discussion groups, but I'd rather join a jacks club any day. The groups that have been important to me one way or another have bypassed the intellect and linked me with other people—usually women—on another level: my childbirth training class, for example, and the Belles Lettres, a women's group that sang show tunes and popular ballads to raise money for the Writers' Room, a New York work space for writers.

Men have known the pleasures of such exclusive groups for centuries. It seems no contradiction to me that I should relish all-female groups yet root for the elimination of all-male groups. They may originally have come into being for purposes as harmless and amusing as jacks, but with the years, they became weighted with power and professional advantage. Perhaps someday women's groups will become pernicious, and men will invoke the force of law to be admitted to the Dukes County Garden Club or the Hatch Road exercise class, but we still have a long way to go.

In the meantime, we had fun barring a man from the Martha's Vineyard jacks tournament. There was, I think, some outrage that a man would want to get in on one of the few things we had to ourselves. As president of a major corporation, he should have lots of other games to play.

TAKING THE WHEEL

When my son Teddy turned sixteen, I taught him how to drive. It was the hardest thing we had done together since he was born.

You might have said, "Send him to driving school." I did! But they teach on cars with automatic transmissions, and I have a stick shift. The driving school got him his license, but the problem of teaching him to drive came back to me.

We spent a lot of time in parking lots. The large one near the tennis courts, with no turns and a long straightaway, was fine for first gear. Day after day Teddy threw the stick into first and tried to ease up on the clutch while gently pushing down on the gas. The car lurched like a buckboard with a broken wheel on a roadbed of rocks. It was so uncomfortable for both of us, we could do only fifteen or twenty minutes at a time. Once I went home seasick.

Helpful words of instruction would not come. Against my will, I fell into the sterile, panicky "Watch out!" or the futile, whiny "Teddy!" How do you tell a person when to release the clutch? How do you explain the degree of pressure necessary on the gas pedal? How could I teach him things I knew in my nerve endings, not in my head?

A friend once taught me the useful word *proprioceptive*. A proprioceptor is a sensory receptor in the muscles, tendons, or joints. My friend used the adjective to refer to the kind of knowledge that took three weeks to convey in words but three hours to acquire if you simply did the thing until it went right. Skiing was his example, but driving would be mine. Driving was something I knew in my proprioceptors: I drove with my legs, not my head. When Teddy learned, it would be because something in his proprioceptors clicked.

Finally, however, I found something useful to say. I noticed that his foot hung in the air after he'd released the clutch. "Don't take your foot all the way off the pedal when you release the clutch. Don't pull up your whole leg. Pivot at the heel." That insight turned out to be key. We were now in first gear, and second was not far behind. As we moved up from parking lots to deserted streets, another conveyable piece of advice sorted itself out from the mass of things I knew in my legs and feet: "Drive on the brake. At low speeds, most of the time you should have your foot on the brake." That insight came after he took a corner at 30 mph. When we first hit traffic, I produced another commandment: "Do not swerve away from oncoming traffic unless it's in your lane."

My own driving deteriorated. As I started to think

about it, I forgot how it was I moved my left and right legs in such graceful, easy coordination, like the centipede who walked very well on his hundred legs until someone marveled, "How do you do that?" "Easy," said the centipede. "I just put one foot here and one foot here," and within five minutes he was tied up in knots.

Teddy was taking it hard. His pride was wounded by his inability to master the car. I kept thinking of him when he was a baby, learning to stand. All day long in his crib he pulled himself up by the bars, fell down, tried again to pull himself up. What resilience! What determination! A baby can do that all day long and never feel embarrassed about failing. He has plenty of time and no self-consciousness. No one, least of all himself, thinks twice about his plopping back onto his mattress. If a baby had to learn to crawl, stand, and walk with a teenager's susceptibility to humiliation, forget it! We'd never leave our bassinets.

Teddy complained that this problem came along just when he felt he was getting good at things. It didn't seem fair. Adult life was almost within his grasp, when suddenly there was the stick shift, raising a new barrier between Youth and Age.

And how did Age feel about it? I mean, leaving aside increased insurance rates and the prospect of constant fear about his safety in the future? It occurred to me that I may not have greeted his achievement of mastery without ambivalence. When he beat me in tennis for the first time, I started thinking a lot about how Age and Experience have to give way eventually to Youth and Strength. I made him play with the wind in his face, and he still beat me, so much stronger was he than I. Give him a car with a stick shift, and what's left for me to do for him? If he can drive himself, soon he will earn his own living, start his own family. Time to toss me out with the biological garbage.

Consciously, I like the idea of passing on my skills and knowledge to the next generation. But how does my mean-spirited unconscious feel? Pass on the skills, and you have passed on your power. The Promethean flame leaves your hands. The life force has used you up, squeezed you dry, needs you no longer. Can it be that all this prevented me from telling Teddy earlier, "Pivot on your heel"?

My only consolation is in knowing that if I were a man, the process of being matched and surpassed by my son would be even more galling, more threatening, would signal even more clearly the waning of my sexual powers.

Shakespeare understood this buried battle for sexual supremacy. What bothers Hamlet? Disgust at his mother for having a boyfriend. She ought to be beyond sex. Time for him now. *The Winter's Tale?* It's about the father's jealousy of the son's youth. Sure, the play says Leontes is jealous of his wife. But look who dies as the result of his fit. Not his wife, but his flirting, sexually precocious son. When the second generation materializes, Leontes has to be reminded that that lady with wrinkles, sculpted by time, is his wife and that the blooming girl he's attracted to is his daughter, and he can't have her. The Macbeths understand best the connection between the failure of power and the rising generations: they want to kill all the children in sight.

Picasso, whose unconscious was as close to the surface as they get, when he was eighty told his teenage son Claude that he wanted no more visits from him. "I am old and you are young," he said, according to his latest biographer. "I wish you were dead."

Of course, the Macbeths were wrong: their only

chance for the immortality they craved was *through* children. Claude Picasso has beaten his father, as most children do, no matter how talented the father, by outliving him. This is the harsh lesson of the life cycle. In the biological long run the only way to retain power is by passing it on. So I was determined, no matter what, to move Teddy into fifth gear, and eventually succeeded.

Soon after, he informed me that, according to what he had learned in driving school, I didn't have enough insurance and should take out an umbrella policy. I checked it out, and he was right. I began to see the glimmering of a better day when I could simply relax and let myself be chauffeured by my son. Of course, that's what King Lear thought, and look what happened to him.

ABOUT THE AUTHOR

Phyllis Rose is the author of *Woman of Letters: A Life of Virginia Woolf*, which was nominated for a National Book Award in 1978; of the acclaimed and enduringly popular *Parallel Lives: Five Victorian Marriages*; and, most recently, of *Jazz Cleopatra: Josephine Baker in Her Time*. She has taught literature at Wesleyan University since 1969, and has written essays, reviews, and articles for many publications, including the "Hers" column in the *New York Times*. She lives in Middletown, Connecticut.